FAMILY PLANNING
AND
POPULATION CONTROL

SOCIAL MOVEMENTS PAST AND PRESENT

Irwin T. Sanders, Editor

FAMILY PLANNING
AND
POPULATION CONTROL

*The Challenges of
a Successful Movement*

Kurt W. Back

Twayne Publishers • Boston
A Division of G. K. Hall & Co.

Family Planning and Population Control:
The Challenges of a Successful Movement
Kurt W. Back

Copyright © 1989 by G. K. Hall & Co.
All rights reserved.
Published by Twayne Publishers
A Division of G. K. Hall & Co.
70 Lincoln Street, Boston, Massachusetts 02111

Copyediting supervised by Barbara Sutton
Book production by Janet Zietowski
Typeset in 10/12 Century Oldstyle
by Compset, Inc., of Beverly, Massachusetts

First Printing 1989

Library of Congress Cataloging-in-Publication Data

Back, Kurt W.
    Family planning and population control : the challenges of a
successful movement / Kurt W. Back.
        p.   cm.—(Social movements past and present)
    Bibliography: p.
    Includes index.
    ISBN 0-8057-9711-4 (alk. paper). ISBN 0-8057-9729-7 (pbk. : alk.
paper)
    1. Birth control.   2. Social movements.   3. Population policy.
I. Title.   II. Series.
HQ766.B143 1989
303.4′84—dc19   88-21786
                                                                            CIP

Contents

About the Author

Kurt W. Back is James B. Duke Professor of Sociology at Duke University. He received his Ph.D. in group psychology at Massachusetts Institute of Technology and has worked at the Bureau of the Census, Columbia University, the University of Puerto Rico, and the University of North Carolina. He was research associate with the Conservation Foundation in Jamaica and has held fellowships at Rockefeller University, St. John's College (Cambridge University), the East-West Center at the University of Hawaii, and the Institute of Population Studies at the University of Exeter. He has published numerous articles, is author of *Slums, Projects and People* and *Beyond Words: The Story of Sensitivity Training and the Encounter Group Movement,* and the co-author of *The Family and Population Control, The Control of Human Fertility in Jamaica,* and other books on aspects and applications of social psychology.

Acknowledgments and
Note on the References

As this is an analytic book on a social movement and uses mainly historical material, no attempt was made to use primary data. References in the text indicate sources consulted; however, no attempt was made to document every statement. Chapter 7 is partly based on my own research and experience.

For the material in chapter 6 on the Rockefeller Far Eastern Mission and the early history of the Population Council, the Rockefeller Archive Center at Pocantico Hills gave gracious permission to use its files and provided generous support for the research; I acknowledge it gratefully. The book was completed at the Institute of Population Studies at the University of Exeter, England, where I stayed during 1987–88, supported by a Senior Research Fellowship of the Fogarty International Center, NIH. I want to thank Dr. Robert Snowden and the staff of the Institute for the warmth and hospitality that made this year so pleasant and productive.

And, as always, to Mary Lou, for making everything worthwhile.

Part 1

The Setting

Chapter One

Introduction

Family planning, birth control, population size, abortion, and right to life figure today among society's most important problems. While individual positions on these topics differ, they are almost universally recognized as vital issues upon which public intervention on one side or another seems unavoidable.

This state of affairs is of quite recent origin. Not that these questions did not exist before, but for a long time they did not come to public consciousness; they were not considered a fit topic for public debate or explicit public policy. Even as recently as the 1940s and 1950s federal support for family planning research, let alone family planning programs, was out of the question; in fact, the few laws that existed were attempts to obstruct the practice or even the discussion of contraception. Similarly, on the international scale, a post–World War II mission to the Far East mentioned the problem of overpopulation, but its recommended solutions included only indirect means, such as collection of better statistics, recruitment of women into the labor force, and general economic improvement. At the time it could hardly be imagined that in the Far East, or in other parts of the world, questions of compulsory family planning or contraception would one day come into the foreground of political discussion. Such a change was as unimaginable then as complete suppression of family planning would seem today.

The speed of this change caught many people by surprise, even those who thought themselves experts on these issues. It had foreseen and unforeseen effects throughout society: on interpersonal relations, on families, on culture, and on the way individuals look at the course of their own lives. The repercussions of this change are still with us and discussion about its significance will continue for a long time. Here we shall concentrate on how the process of this transformation occurred. The story is interesting in itself; but its unique features give us insight into the larger patterns of social change in general, and it helps us understand a particular kind of social movement—namely one that is based on increases in knowledge and technology. It must be stressed, however, that the fate of these innovations in society is so dependent on the underlying social conditions that we are faced here with a social phenomenon, not a technical development (Back 1987).

As an introduction to this topic, this chapter provides an overview of the increased scientific and technical progress on the one side and changing social norms and social actions on the other. Following is a discussion of the specific conditions of the problem of family planning and population control and a consideration of how the family planning movement thereby deviated from the standard course taken by social movements. These preliminaries will help to establish the setting for a discussion of the family planning movement and its allies and opponents within the frame of socially innovative movements.

Social Change and Social Movement

Social change seems to happen when the conditions are ripe, often when some technical advance has dislocated current arrangements, when unforeseen events have brought in a new factor. Looking at events in retrospect, one can be easily convinced that some innovations are just reasonable reactions to a new problem. But while people are living in unstable situations many new directions seem open; which one will be taken cannot be predicted merely from a rational analysis of the problem.

Social transformations do not arrive by themselves, but some conditions are helpful and some are obstacles to change. In order to show how a society was led to certain changes, one must first describe such underlying conditions as prevailing tensions, the need for their correction, and new insights gained in scientific progress. In many cases movement occurs so gradually and with so little perceptible argument that no specific individuals or groups can be held responsible for it. In other conditions, however, more than one course is possible and different protagonists struggle for different solutions.

Very often the kind of solution that is finally accepted for social difficulties depends on the efforts of a few individuals and organized groups. These efforts coalesce into social movements, long-term organized formations that try to effect particular change. Social movements come in many ways and shapes; their study forms a separate branch of sociology. Much past research has focused on the internal workings of these movements: how they are directed, how they function, how leaders and different kinds of participants are distinguished. Scholars have therefore concentrated mainly on the larger movements: those that have imposing aims to reconstitute or renew society and to eliminate a variety of ills, and which require intense devotion from their followers.

Social movements can target either society's values or its technical knowledge. Most past movements have attacked values, because of their emotional power. Conversely, technical knowledge arouses little feeling. We can understand that people who are unwilling to change their religious convictions may be willing to fight or die for them; at the same time they might adopt a "better mousetrap" if they are persuaded of its better function. Thus, for the adoption of many technical innovations we do not speak of a social movement, but of dissemination of a new technique or device. In describing the introduction of these innovations, we would not speak of the principles of social movements but of the simple process of reasonable persuasion, demonstration of superior methods, and similarly reasoned actions. We would not expect people to become emotional about a better way of heating their homes, for example, despite advertisers' attempt to create feelings of this kind among the users of their products.

The distinction between the two processes—changes in technical knowledge and changes in values—is not so clear as one might suppose. Social movements may claim to have bases in incontrovertible facts, and weak rational arguments for the spread of technical innovations may be bolstered by using emotional pressures. Practically all social movements claim, to some degree, bases in logic and reason; spread of new information usually also relies on socially normative claims. Sometimes innovations are more based on social scientific knowledge than on that of the "hard" sciences. Examples would be social indicators or encounter groups, which are social technologies, but which have given rise to corresponding movements. Thus, movements that depend at least partially on the insights of social science illustrate the blurred line between value transformation and the transmission of technical knowledge, because they try to change human behavior and consciousness, but employ technical advances for their purpose.

The family planning movement shows these two processes—technical innovation and values change—at work and demonstrates how they interweave. On the one hand, rapid population increase gave occasion for fear that an excess in the human race would exhaust the resources of the earth. In addition, there was a growing concern about the consequences that excessive childbearing had on women, children, and the quality of life of families, especially in urban slums. On the other hand, medical knowledge about procreation and the means of contraception increased with the growth in scientific knowledge of the human reproductive system. Thus people searching for solutions to a variety of social problems found hopes in the new technology.

The history of the family planning movement also shows the complications in this dual process. Not only did the change in values—from high fertility to low fertility—arouse heated discussion, but the new techniques were not looked at as purely rational tools but as value-laden devices. The questions of what could be done and what should be done were confounded. Different points of view developed about the means and ends of population control. There was no automatic change, resolving the social strain with the aid of the new scientific technique. Different solutions were possible and the actions of prominent individuals and organizations made a great difference in the outcome.

The actual course that the introduction of family planning into society has taken was largely determined by several social currents. These currents followed their own patterns, partly determined by their own dynamics, partly by the nature of population control and family planning issues.

A social movement is a response to a need that society does not fill for a number of its members. Awareness of this need may arise because of recently changed circumstances or because some people have become conscious of a long-standing condition. Sociological theorists have determined that several factors are essential for the progress and success of a social movement. Neil Smelser (1963) isolated five factors: *structural conduciveness,* the openness of channels for action within the existing structure; *strain,* conditions that show the incapacity of existing systems to satisfy certain needs; *generalized beliefs,* which indicate some diagnosis for the failure and proposals for eventual solution; *precipitating events,* which dramatize both the strain and possible avenues of adjustment; and finally, *social control,* the measure in which the existing system can contain and channel the emerging movement.

A specific sequence of events was identified by Herbert Blumer

(1946): *unrest,* where people are becoming susceptible to new appeals; *popular excitement,* an agreement on the causes of the difficulty and sharpening of the objectives; *indoctrination,* the emergence of a definite set of beliefs and of mechanisms, such as leadership, to disseminate them, and finally *institutionalization,* when the purposes of the movements are carried out.

Besides these general steps abstracted by scholars, social movements have their particular stories of rise, success, and fall; they also reveal general patterns. First, there is a time before a movement gets underway when conditions are very bad, but nobody can quite say what the problem is, much less what can be done about it. Next, there is a period when a few early heroes identify issues and assemble some followers, usually not enough to have an impact. These persons are later looked upon as the ancestors of the movement, frequently also as martyrs. In modern terms, what the early leaders do is "consciousness raising." Then, as the issues involved are identified, various schools of thought develop, with either different aspects of the problem considered or different solutions proposed. If the movement is to advance, there is an amalgamation of these views, usually under strong leadership. At that point the movement proper is born and ready to fight for its aims. Its mythology then includes heroes and heroines, struggles and suffering, victories and defeats, internal and external conflicts. Finally, the moment occurs when the movement has achieved its aims (or given them up, if it was unsuccessful). Its achievement may turn out to be different from the original dreams, but the movement has to adjust to its new, dominant position. When its aims become the new status quo, excesses and conflicts will arise; new groups will start within the movement; and new opponents can capitalize on unrest and unmet needs. Decline or stagnation sets in, and the chapter is closed.

Inquiry into a specific social movement combines the abstract, almost mathematical, analysis of steps that are common to all social movements with the vivid history that the movement—and its opponents—have generated as a mythology that holds the faithful together. The chapters that follow tell the story of the family planning movement, its ideas, events, heroes, heroines, and villains. For the most part this story stays within the framework of the general processes of social movements. The remainder of the chapter deals with attributes of the questions of population control and family planning that gave the movement its particular nature and history. The next two chapters deal with the two principal sources from which the movement derived: the demographic and economic concerns with overpopulation, and the welfare concern with women and children and the standard of living for families. The following chapters consider the evolution of these concerns into the family planning movement, its heroic period, and its sudden triumph. Later chapters study the implications of this triumph, in national and international spheres. They pinpoint the results institutionalization and nationalization of family planning has had in many countries. The final chapters consider new sources of conflict: the abortion controversy, the right-to-life movement, and the new questioning of the basic premises of the family planning movement. There can now be speculation about the enduring consequences of the movement and the social processes and movements that may spring up out of the new situation.

Humanity and Human Nature

Population policy leads eventually to a peculiar question: should there be more of us, or fewer? What this "us" means depends on the questioner, but the very question implies that a group of people can be increased and decreased for some ultimate purpose. (For instance, some economists say that if there were fewer people they would be better off than if there were more people.) A completely opposing view point holds that each individual is unique and one cannot add or subtract human beings for any purpose. Few people hold the extreme of either point of view, but most are influenced by one or the other to some degree.

One cannot easily decide between these two positions. Any answer will depend on a complex of other values, which ultimately connect to the meaning of human life. Religion and personal philosophy will guide one's attitudes: What is the meaning of an individual life? Can one person decide about the value of another's life? Is every life worth living? What are one's duties to the community? These questions are rarely considered precisely in this form, but, if pressed, people can give answers to these questions of ultimate concern, which guide action in many fields.

Fertility control is such a central question because procreation is the basis of the existence of the human race and of every particular society. Fertility control programs have to consider, in addition to issues of religious and personal philosophy, the ways in which the different species find their place in nature and control their relative abundance (population biology). All species, including *Homo sapiens,* reach, through evolution and adaptation, the population size that is the largest possible for their environment. Mass disasters are rare because species have developed mechanisms to avoid overpopulation and to maintain equilibrium. In the human species, biological controls are supplemented and often replaced by social mechanisms, but the loss of many natural restraints sometimes produces population dislocations that cannot adapt quickly to social changes.

Any species tends to increase to the maximum of available resources and thus an increase in population means that a particular species has found a better way to use its environment. This point of view is represented in many common social and cultural values. In our language, the words *growth, expansion,* and *increase* have positive values. Cities vie to show increase from census to census and demand recounts if population increase is not as large as they expect. This may be due partly to reasons of political power and economic advantage, but simple civic pride is often a factor. The emotional satisfaction of belonging to a large unit can play an important role. This link has an ancient heritage. Legend, myth, and history are full of examples of promises of increase in offspring, which is considered highly desirable. There are a few examples of population groups limiting their own size as a desired goal.

It is against this overwhelming tradition that promotion of a goal of population limitation must fight. Individuals, especially women, may admit to suffering from unwanted pregnancies, yet be reluctant to advocate a general goal of comparative sterility, of families without children, or of population decline. In language and in everyday behavior, even most advocates of population control prefer growth to sterility, rise to decline, and will rejoice in a new baby. It is difficult for members of a family planning movement to find an acceptable mode of behavior, one that reflects honestly their values and is not offensive to the general population or even to themselves.

Acceptability of Methods

The aims of population control touch on a wide range of deep-seated, but seldom expressed emotions. These feelings come also into play in the means that are advocated to reach movement goals. In the final analysis population control is achieved through the personal control of reproduction. The reproductive process can be divided into three phases, in each of which control is possible: intercourse, conception, and gestation (Davis and Blake 1956). Population planning can involve any of these steps; opposition to each method will depend on social values, from protection of privacy in programs to reduce intercourse to protection of the fetus in methods involving interruption of gestation. The family planning movement brought the discussion of population control into the open. A discussion ensued over the acceptability of different methods according to various moral values: whether the methods are natural, whether they are humanly possible, and whether they interfere with the human rights of the infant and of the parents. Even if family planners can avoid the question of a definite policy on population size—emphasizing individual control over family size instead—the question of the permissibility of different means inevitably leads to conflict.

In the history of the family planning movement, opposition has come from different sources; some are opposed to the aim and some to the means. Similarly, different wings of the movement have advocated either population control through social regulation, family restriction through direct regulation, or reliance on individual free choice, given the means. For example, Marxists, focusing on the aims of the movement, have seen the concern with overpopulation as an indication of maldistribution, which would be remedied by economic reforms, but Marxists are little concerned with the specific means of family planning. By contrast, the Catholic church, focusing on the means of the movement, recognizes the danger of overpopulation and of excessively large families but opposes most contraceptive methods, which it considers unnatural and immoral. The family planning movement has had to fight these two social forces on extremely different grounds.

Indirect and Direct Methods

Family planning touches on so many sensitive issues that it seems reasonable to ask whether the goal of population control could not be reached in a different way. Demographic history has shown that families have become smaller, the general birthrate has dropped, and population increase has subsided when certain social changes have occurred. Among these are various aspects of modernization, such as urban living, increase in education, women's entrance into the labor force, drop in infant mortality, and general increase of living standards. Many people have found it reasonable to assume that promoting these generally accepted characteristics of modernization would in the long run produce the same results that the family planning movement has tried to achieve by promoting contraception. People who encourage certain aspects of modernization as goals in themselves have tried to convince family planners that planning would occur spontaneously if their own goals—such as women's rights or industrialization—were achieved.

The possibility of achieving population control without actually advocating it has looked enticing. In addition, many people involved in the family planning movement have also been sympathetic with the aims of the other groups, sometimes being actively involved in several groups at the same time. Traditionally, family planning has been part of a coalition of activists of general liberal orientation, supporting civil rights, social reforms, women's rights, and legislation that combines all these aims.

Trust in the automatic effect of general social change has its own problems for the family planning movement. In demographic history there have been many surprising changes. People who see population reduction as a prime necessity have become cautious about advocating developments that may or may not lead to fertility control. For those who believe the population problem is urgent, policies that have long-range and uncertain effects seem too hesitant and slow an approach to the immediate crisis.

These considerations show, however, that one cannot look at family planning in isolation. In order to understand the alliances and conflicts of the family planning movement one has to consider the whole array of related issues that may influence fertility control.

Summary: The Place of a Social Movement

In recent social history many important changes in population control have occurred. Many of them might have happened naturally, but others reflect the efforts of organized groups. Most theories on population agree that fertility decline accompanies the kind of technical, economic, and social changes that have occurred within the last centuries. But credit (or blame) for population decline must also go to the persons and groups that advocated fertility control in the family planning movement. Like any other movement, family planning acquired a special identity, with its own aims, organization, leadership, recruitment, and relations to the world at large. It also has special characteristics, arising from the particular nature of its concerns: its conjunction with biological drives, with very private matters, with the needs of the community, and with religious and philosophical values put it in direct contact and possible conflict with many other aspects of society. Thus, in tracing the story of the movement, we must concern ourselves with the social setting, the general knowledge of physiological facts in the population and the social condition of population planning, as well as the personalities of the leaders and the historical accidents that determined the direction of the movement, its branches, allies, and opponents.

Chapter Two

The Social Background

Social movements arise out of ambiguous and tense situations. Just as on a small scale a "milling around" stage occurs before a riot breaks out, so an equivalent unrest can be seen in the intellectual and social climate before a social movement originates. The identification of new problems, new claims of remedies, and the adoption of new techniques show this loosening of accepted standards and questioning of old certainties. In the family planning movement only a minor part of society was involved, and for the most part the movement did not advocate a total upheaval of values or violent action. Changes in technical knowledge were an essential prerequisite for its emergence.

The Tradition

Systematic concern with overpopulation has a short history. People have been aware for generations of drawbacks of too large a population concentration, and societies have adapted by different processes to provide some regulations, including inheritance laws, especially of land through primogeniture in feudal society; mechanisms for delay of marriage—for instance, through limitation of new houses in preindustrial society; provision for celibate occupations, with especially high value given to religious vocation in the Middle Ages; and traditions of migration. It is rare, however, to find direct statements that too many people of one's own kind constitute a calamity. Population restrictions were usually directed toward others.

The purposive dissemination of contraception also has a short history. Techniques of birth control have been known since ancient times (Himes 1936), but until recently systematic knowledge was practically non-existent and restricted to a small faction. The most common methods were abortion and coitus interruptus, but neither of them can be considered systematic methods of family planning. Mechanical and even chemical methods were transmitted by tradition within families; some rudimentary ideas could be found in medical publications. But, in essence, technical knowledge was based on unsystematic methods that were thought to be useful. Further advance was limited by the lack of systematic scientific knowledge about the human reproductive system. It was even more inhibited by cultural restraints: widespread knowledge was supposed to promote promiscuity and other forbidden sexual behavior and the standard knowledge of the time was therefore withheld from the people to whom it could be ultimately useful. Contraception was mainly a surreptitious, slightly disreputable practice. This reputation probably discouraged serious professionals from engaging themselves in the field.

Attitudes toward population and contraception at the beginning of the industrial revolution were still represented largely by the biblical injunction: Be fruitful and multiply. Only in special cases did people try consciously to restrict population increase or to limit the sizes of individual families. But by the beginning of the nineteenth century values in favor of family planning were introduced and knowledge about contraception became more widespread.

Expansion of Knowledge on Population

The eighteenth century, the Age of Reason, encouraged curiosity in all directions. Budding scientific interest led first to making inventories about the facts of human life: how many people live in different places, how they are distributed in households, at what rate they are born and at what rate they die. Collection of these facts had been undertaken before for practical uses, for instance, tax collection and the military draft, and for this reason was sometimes resisted (Glass 1973). But now many researchers became interested in these numbers for their own sake and developed the first procedures for systematic collection of population data. This effort fit in with the general spirit of the time, a spirit of inquiry in which amateur scientists collected a wealth of data and started to look for systems of classification and analysis.

With the same spirit scholars looked at comparative data from history and from different societies. They saw the rise and fall of different societies and empires. They noticed the increases and declines in numbers and looked for their varied causes. From their point of view—and they lived in era of colonial expansion—an increasing or at least a static society seemed the ideal; decline in numbers was considered to be a sign of a decline in morals and social stamina (Eversley 1959). Many writers blamed the moral degeneracy caused by luxury for population decline and loss of national strength, taking their cue from the decline of the Roman Empire. They studied the writings of Roman writers who had warned their contemporaries of this fate. The sterile soft life of the upper classes was contrasted with the fertility of the proletarians (which literally means: the people who contribute to the state through their offspring); only through the help of the latter could the military and commercial needs of expansion be met.

The collection of hard data that could supplant vague generalizations about the benefits of population change began in the seventeenth century. John Graunt (1662) analyzed bills of death (mortality records) and demonstrated regularity in seemingly random processes, suggesting that further such investigations would be valuable. Graunt's work and that of his eighteenth-century successors laid the groundwork for the scientific endeavor later called demography. The systematic collection of data and the observation of regular patterns in the seemingly arbitrary events of birth, death, and population size led people to consider the possibility of influencing these patterns.

If one can understand an event, one can start to think about controlling it. By the end of the eighteenth century social philosophers started to question the traditional wisdom of the virtue of expansion and the evil of population decline. The limits of natural resources became apparent, perhaps because the completion of the basic geographic discoveries promoted a global consciousness. People stopped seeing themselves as living in a spot in the middle of possibly limitless unknown land, and started to realize the limits of land and natural resources. Gradually attention shifted from concerns of depopulation through luxury, to those of overpopulation through irresponsibility. The blame shifted from the soft upper classes to the lower classes for producing children for which neither they nor the society could provide.

Population Values

Scientific discovery alone does not cause social action. A stronger stimulus must be present to precipitate disruption of existing social arrangements. We find such a stimulus in the last decades of the eighteenth century and the beginning of the nineteenth. Advances in technology, especially in the production of food and in public hygiene, decreased the death rate of infants so much that the same fertility led to an increase in population; furthermore, these developments made concentration in cities possible, increasing urban size and density (McKeown 1976). This, in turn, encouraged industries with their large factories and huge working forces. Disruption was caused by three kinds of shift in population: absolute increase in population, rural-to-urban residential shift, and agricultural-to-industrial occupational shift. These changes led to a profound upheaval in the quality of life for many: population density usually meant an accumulation of slum dwellings, urban conglomeration and the new patterns of employment changed the timing and manner in which families could be formed; above all, these changes in the lives of the poor made them more visible; slums and back alleys in cities were seen by many more of the affluent than the more dispersed poverty in the countryside. The crowding together of so many individuals and families with similar problems also made them more conscious of their own status. Both the disruption itself and the attention given to it became important in the population movement.

The previous natural checks on fertility and those provided by rural social organization weakened in the new arrangement. In rural areas marriage was only possible when a new home was available; building a new home required substantial resources and long preparation. More often new households were formed when a home became available through death, migration, or retirement. Unmarried children could then live in their parents' household, go into private service, or leave the community, such as entering military or naval service, or moving to cities (Laslett 1985). Large cities with their high density became attractive destinations for unmarried rural men and women. Traditional housing limitations for families, which had precluded excessive family formation in rural areas, were thus abolished. Similarly, the limitations imposed on a family's size by the capacity of the farm to support it were removed in the city, which was supplied from outside through improved agricultural production. The possibility of employment for young unmarried people, even at the low wages of early industry, made earlier independence from the family possible. Social controls of premarital and extramarital intercourse that had prevailed in the rural areas were removed. Because of the new conditions infant mortality declined and more children lived to the age at which they themselves could form families. All this contributed to sudden increase in population in confined areas where a population explosion could be felt almost physically.

The pressure of large families, the influence of frequent births on the life chances of their mothers and fathers, and crowding and oppressive living conditions marked the population dislocation, which is still apparent in the slum areas of newly exploding cities of developing countries. The age-old types of controls, similar to the natural controls of all species, were failing, and people were led to look for consciously planned controls in their place.

The economic and demographic dislocations were bases for vaguely felt unrest. Although many people were materially better off, they lived in new unaccustomed situations without the comfortable routines and social supports that had endured over long periods. For many, the move to the city and wage work gave the hope of economic advancement for themselves or for their offspring. But conditions were still hard and relief uncertain. New social classes formed, and class consciousness arose in some quarters. Many movements for radical changes, revolutions, and utopias arose during this time. Socialism, nationalism, anarchism, Chartism, abolitionism, and universal suffrage were only a few of the causes that aroused popular interest. All these groups had in common a desire for change, adapting to and even transcending the new economic conditions that the decline of the old regime, based on land ownership and agriculture, had produced. Sometimes these advocates of particular changes worked in common, sometimes independently, and sometimes they competed against each other. Large-scale ideological movements tried to make a consistent system of all the different strains and produce an overarching ideology. These resulted in the great violent movements of the twentieth century. We shall deal later with some of the representatives of these movements who became important in family planning.

Malthus and His Opponents

The sources of unrest combined with the newly found knowledge to translate discussion into action. The Age of Reason gave way to the age of revolution. People acted on their ideas, and serious considerations of the consequences of isolated ideas became necessary. Although population problems were not at the center of the social upheaval of the time, they were bound to come into the general discussion. It was in this setting that English economist Thomas Robert Malthus, the most prominent exponent of population control in the early nineteenth century, emerged. His influence is still felt today.

Malthus's entry into the field was occasioned by the work of William Godwin. Godwin's book, *Enquiry concerning Political Justice and Its Influence on Morals and Happiness* (1793), was intended as a radical remedy to poverty and to general deprivation of the lower classes. His ideas were utopian and could be attacked on this ground. But, Malthus, in his *Essay on Population* (1798), did not attack the practicality of Godwin's manifesto, arguing instead that the aim itself was unrealistic. He claimed that improvement of the status of the poor was self-defeating, because increase in the birth rate of the poor would negate all social gains. The issue was joined. The ensuing debate elaborated the economic positions that are still the basic stances of the opponents in population debate. Malthus and his adversaries defined the new sciences of demography and economics.

Like many of the departures in the birth of new sciences, Malthus's ideas had been stated before, but he gave these ideas legitimacy by assembling impressive evidence from many sources and then using this copious data to show the possible limits of natural resources and, consequently, of possible human expansion.

In his work he opposed both the traditional economic view of his time, namely mercantilism, and new utopian aims promoted in the revolutionary atmosphere. Mercantilism was a system advocated by the leaders of the developing national states in Europe who were starting to strengthen their military and political power by industrial development. The policy of the mercantilists was to protect their own industries from competition, subsidize their growth, and expand the domestic market through aggressive trade and even more aggressive military efforts, leading to colonial expansion or at least to favorable, exclusive, trade agreements. This policy worked well for the countries that started it, especially France under Louis XIV, whose finance minister, Colbert, was one of the first advocates of this policy. The more additional countries adopted these policies and tried to gain strength in this way, the more this policy became self-limiting and led to conflict; wars during this time, between France, Spain, England, and the Netherlands especially, were to some extent caused by one country's attempting to impose its mercantile advantage over the other. Another attack on the system came when the colonial possessions objected to the restrictions imposed by the mercantilistic regime; the American Revolution was the model reaction to the trade restrictions by the European mercantilistic powers and served as a warning to the limits of the system.

Mercantilistic restrictions and other traditions inherited from even earlier times came to be seen as unreasonable burdens. Several new intellectual and political movements tried to assert new ways that would increase human prosperity without obnoxious restrictions. Two of these approaches became important to the discussion of population (Petersen 1979). One adopted the abolition of restraints on production and trade, relying on market forces to assure optimum efficiency; this position was formulated by Adam Smith and was elaborated as laissez-faire liberalism. The other involved a complete reorganization of society and the power structure to produce a state in which the welfare of all was guaranteed; this was expressed in part by Jean-Jacques Rousseau's writings and elaborated in detail by such writers as Godwin; it became the forerunner of various strands of socialism. Neither approach originally gave the population question a central or even an important position.

Thomas Malthus put the population question in the forefront of economic discussion. Malthus opposed the reformers who thought that a rearrangement of power and property would eliminate all poverty and distress. He accepted the fact that the restrictions imposed by the old regime on the free flow of trade also impeded the full expression of economic opportunities. But he defended those social regulations that promoted the industrial and trade developments of early nineteenth-century England. In contrast to other laissez-faire economists he did not propose that this free trade expansion would lead to prosperity for all, nor did he feel constrained to design new regulations that would lead to this result. On the contrary, he proposed a natural law according to which population would always expand to the ultimate limits of natural resources; he specified this relation by trying to show that population expands in a geometric progression and resources in an arithmetic progression; thus population would always outrun available food supplies. Malthus bolstered this hypothesis by data showing the expansion of human populations without restraint; for this he used the available statistics from the nascent United States of America, which was at the time ideally situated for expansion. He compared these data with the availability of food resources and the possibilities for expanded land cultivation, thus demonstrating that the opportunities for developing new food sources are limited even under ideal conditions.

From this Malthus concluded that human welfare programs were self-defeating. Policies that would radically improve the status of the poor would always be followed by expansion of the population until people again would be close to the starvation level. Hence any directed improvement of society would end in misery. Malthus did not really see much chance for large-scale improvement; hence economics, which sprang in great part from his analysis, was dubbed the "gloomy science."

In the first edition of his work Malthus concentrated on the evidence for his basic principle, that population would tend to rise to the limits of subsistence. He realized, however, that population does not do so in most existing countries and in the second edition of his work, in 1803, he started to explain why this was so, making possible policy recommendations. He introduced here a number of checks on population expansion, positive checks, which increased mortality, and preventive checks, which reduced fertility. The positive checks, which include war, disease, and famine, serve as a warning of the outcome of unrestricted population expansion. He divided the preventive checks into two kinds, vice, which included promiscuity, homosexuality, adultery, and contraception; and moral restraint, namely delayed marriage, voluntary celibacy, and abstinence in marriage. Moral restraint among prudent people was his main recommendation for avoiding the dire effects of overpopulation. Notice, however, that he classified contraception as "vice" (Petersen 1979).

In general, Malthus's pessimistic conclusion was that nature would keep humanity on a subsistence level, with some starvation to take care of the excess. He opposed any restructuring of society or even welfare measures because tampering with nature would only increase the numbers of the poor and increase misery. Implied in this view is an acceptance of the earlier population theorists. Luxury would decrease fertility—which in his case was an argument for luxury—and the poor were irresponsible and improvident and would always breed to capacity.

Needless to say, Malthus's ideas were not unchallenged. The incipient industrial revolution produced appalling conditions, but it also showed ways for greater productivity and improved nutrition. The expansion of cultivation outside Europe and advances in fertilization and general agriculture occurred just at that time and made a pessimistic view of the limits of subsistence quite unpopular. The opposition to Malthus can be divided in two groups. One, represented by Malthus's friend Nassau Senior (1826), elaborated Adam Smith's view that technical advancement, if unfettered by state regulation, would keep productivity ahead of population expansion: under these conditions population increase and prosperity would go hand in hand. Radical reformers on the other hand claimed that the system of production, not an iron law of nature, was responsible for misery. This view, particularly influenced by Rousseau and espoused by Karl Marx and Friedrich Engels, became the official doctrine of Marxist socialism; it was extremely critical of Malthus and painted him in the darkest colors (Meek 1953). He was seen as an apologist for an unjust system and as promoting the inevitability of poverty in order to protect the currently rich. Marx did admit in his *Critique of the Gotha Program* (1875) that there would be no hope for social improvement if Malthus's population principle were correct (which he saw as possible), but he saw sufficient evidence that revolutionary collective action would bring about a better world. An allied criticism, also deriving from Rousseau, came from writers who romanticized the poor and who objected mainly to demographers' procedure of reducing persons to numbers and in this way salvaging the conscience of the rich. A strong representative of this view is Charles Dickens whose *Oliver Twist* and *Hard Times* are vivid attacks on such quantification of suffering (Frank 1984).

These three points of view, the tragic necessity of nature, the benign view of natural social development, and the solution of population problems through radical social change, have persisted as the principal orientations toward population increase in political economics and its successor, the politics of population. We shall see later how these perspectives color current discussions. One aspect, however, was missing. All the writers discussed the general conditions of population increase and its advisability; they did not treat in detail what could be done to control fertility. Sexual relations or even life in families were not discussed as a part of the population problem.

Technical Advances in Family Planning

While the scholars in the rising sciences of demography and economics discussed the consequences of different population sizes and densities, new advances in the means achieving population limitation came from different sources. Changes in values and knowledge led to the start of family planning as a feasible enterprise. Important among these changes were the increasing understanding of the process of reproduction and the dissemination of effective techniques for birth control.

It is hard to realize what the state of knowledge and technology was in this field a scant two centuries ago. People knew more and less at that time than we might suppose (Fryer 1965). On the one hand, the rudiments of practically all current techniques (with the important exception of hormonal methods—i.e., the contraceptive pill) had been in use since ancient times. The knowledge was not systematic, however, and was transmitted in different traditions in a scattered way. People frequently did not know why techniques worked; effective methods and superstitions were given equal weight.

On the other hand, the knowledge of the biology of reproduction was very primitive; it was not until the end of the eighteenth century that the exact nature of the male and female contribution to conception in the human species was established. These two strands of necessary information—contraceptive techniques and knowledge of reproduction—were not coordinated. Medical training was not formal education but personal experience, preferably apprenticeship with a senior physician (Starr 1982). It did not include much academic training in anatomical and physiological bases of reproduction, a field about which little was known and even less was talked about. It is not surprising therefore that the same devices were used for enhancing fertility and for contraception and that many writings by physicians were more moral exhortations than hypotheses and prescriptions on how to prevent conception (Himes 1936).

Information on this topic was so scattered in different sources that it is still unclear whether progress in contraception during this time consisted of better application of well-known practices or greater dissemination of knowledge and development of newer, more reliable techniques (Lesthaege 1977). The basic principles of birth control were known to some specialists, but radically new ideas in the field did not arise until the 1950s. Technical developments made contraceptives safer, more convenient to use, and more effective; in particular, the invention of vulcanized rubber in the late nineteenth century made the condom and diaphragm much more effective. On the other hand, large groups of the population were ill-informed about available methods and had no idea how to obtain information. Even relatively well-informed physicians frequently felt it their duty to prevent the spread of knowledge about contraception; they appeared to be more concerned about the moral effects of knowledge than about the medical effects of ignorance.

We can appreciate the frustration felt by reformers who were upset by the results of overpopulation and large families, who knew that means were available to control fertility, but that they were withheld from the people who needed them. The discrepancy between perceived need and available means appeared so large that much effort was devoted simply to making contraceptive means available to large population groups. In fact, the fight against informal restrictions and legal obstacles to the existing techniques forms the most impressive part of the early population control movement. The incipient family planning movement concentrated on dissemination of existing knowledge. Support of new methods came much later.

Changing Values in Family Size

We cannot reconstruct completely the change in family and personal values that occurred in the late eighteenth and early nineteenth centuries. Similar changes are occurring today, however, in less developed countries where fertility decrease is just starting. Although these events are not replications of earlier events in the West, conditions are sufficiently similar that research into the current situation can give us insight into earlier conditions, especially concerning the problem of family limiting and direct questioning of individuals.

A number of studies have been done on the value of children in several societies. Data has been obtained from questionnaires that focus on gratifications that people get from having children and on their costs (Bulatao 1979, Fawcett 1983). Investigators have found that the motives for having children can be divided into three groups: economic gains and costs, rewarding interactions, which include companionship and fun with children and effects on the marital bond, and psychological appreciation, which includes identification with offspring and fulfillment in shaping them. Initially, in high-fertility, mainly agricultural societies, the worth of children is weighed in terms of economic contribution and cost. With the rise of cities and industrial employment, family units become smaller and economic factors less important. Interaction with children and the personality of the child itself assume a salient role. Rewarding and nonrewarding interactions have important features; the family turns inward, placing emphasis on each individual child. An interest in the conjugal family unit and in the fortunes of individual members leads to concern about controlling the fate of the family, including the size of the unit. The family then becomes receptive to the idea of control and the techniques for achieving it.

The changes in the nature of the family and increased value of children, observed in developing countries can also be found in the eighteenth and nineteenth centuries. Evidence indicates an increased interest in children and a recognition of children as special persons (Ariès 1962). Before this period children had not been considered as essentially different from adults. They were smaller, weaker, and less knowledgeable in many ways, but those were deficiencies that might exist among adults. The place of children was therefore not different from that of adults of diminished competence; they could participate in society as far as they were able and their station in life permitted. They had to learn the skills needed for proper functioning, but teaching these skills was not considered to be a specialized branch of social activity as education is today, and the family was not seen as responsible for making education available. Children fit gradually into their proper role as adults, accepting training and contributing their share in the meantime. No particular provision had to be made for their special condition.

Only in the eighteenth century did the idea take hold that children had separate needs and potentialities. New theories of education and of treatment of children developed, among the most prominent of which were Rousseau's. Schools and even preschools for the very young were introduced. Children were no longer just a minor part of the household but a separate responsibility with recognized needs different from those of the adult members. In the allocation of resources—money, time, or emotional involvement—the individual child needed a larger share. The greater expenditures necessary for each child led to concern about limiting the total number of children in a family.

Added to these considerations was the incipient decline of mortality and especially of child mortality, which again was partially due to greater concern with the individual's nutrition, hygiene, and health. When the assumption had been that a family had to produce a large number of children in order to ensure the survival of a few, a comparatively small emotional investment was made in each child. Now interest in each child's development and the greater likelihood that it would survive contributed to the awakening emphasis on smaller families.

In fact, the birth rate started to decline in some parts of Western Europe in the eighteenth century, but not enough to put a noticeable dent in the population increase; mortality decreased more quickly (Coale and Watkins 1985). Nevertheless, first in France and then in England a decrease in family size occurred, especially among the higher economic classes where changes in the treatment of children had become noticeable. In France the upper-class tradition had been to send infants to wet nurses in the country and to keep them there through childhood; this kept the interest in individual children and the investment in time and emotion low; the cost of this upbringing was relatively small compared to the parent's income. Toward the end of the eighteenth century interest in the new theories of education made parents more inclined to keep their children at home: families became smaller as interest in children increased. A similar process occurred in England in the next century (Banks 1954). Cost for schooling and maintenance increased from the beginning to the end of the nineteenth century, partly as a consequence of educational reform in private as well as publicly supported schools. Again new theories of educational and moral development were responsible. In addition, new special training was needed to provide administrators for an expanding empire and its cost put a new financial burden on middle- and upper-class parents. Malthus himself taught at a college preparing the employees of the East India Company and was responsible for better and more elaborate training. The increased responsibilities and cost led to fewer children per family.

Conclusion

The accumulation of obstacles that lay in the way of family planning started to break up at the end of the eighteenth century. In knowledge as well as in values, in concern with the fate of nations as well as with individuals and their families, new departures replaced old settled conditions. The universally held virtue of population increase was doubted and figures were assembled to settle the issue; information on family planning started to be discussed and hints appeared that the persons who were ultimately concerned with childbearing were entitled to the basic facts. The romantic emphasis on the worth of the individual, buttressed by declining infant mortality, gave value to the individual child, and quality came to supplant quantity in family planning.

These gradual changes came almost imperceptively until they could not be ignored. In terms of the processes described in Chapter One, society started to show strain in respect to family planning (Smelser

1963), and the unrest preliminary to popular arousal became apparent (Blumer 1946). In terms of the typical stories of social improvements, this is the situation where strong individuals, willing to work devotedly for changes, can arise, giving the original direction to a social movement; the next chapters will tell their story in the family planning campaign.

Part 2

The Heroic Age

Chapter Three

Rebels and Radicals

The nineteenth century has been called the age of ideology. Perhaps it should better be called the age of unlimited possibilities. The political, scientific, and industrial revolutions that occurred at the turn of the century abolished old certainties. Social changes had shown that the customary mutual obligations were just that, customary, but not necessary, norms. In addition, new practices were found to be technically possible, and immutable natural laws started to be doubted or replaced.

Politically, the turn of the century had been dominated first by the French Revolution, starting in 1789, and then the rise and fall of its outgrowth, the Napoleonic empire. The reaction that set in upon the final defeat of Napoleon at Waterloo in 1815 was an attempt to re-create the life of the eighteenth century, but it was only outwardly successful. Old beliefs had been shattered. People could conform to old norms, but they had learned that new social and intellectual arrangements were possible. The feudal system of inherited status gave way to a ranking based on acquired wealth and personal ability; Napoleon himself had presided over a revision of the Civil Code that stressed family responsibility for the advancement of children. The creation of new societies and even new individuals was seen as possible; such an environment was indeed fertile ground for all kind of new ideas.

Some of them led to new cults and utopian groups, such as Fourierism and Saint-Simonism; others, which had mainly rational bases, started new sciences: Malthus, Senior, and David Ricardo founded political economics, and Auguste Comte founded sociology. At the same time, some of the ideas coalesced and inspired social movements. Intellectual leaders formed a very small percentage of a small population and were therefore likely to be in contact with each other. People with common interests and concerns quickly found each other, making contacts even across national boundaries.

Francis Place

Among these intellectual leaders was the first proponent of change who combined the growing concern over economic and family conditions with advocacy of birth control (Reed 1978, Wallas 1918). Francis Place was born in London in 1759 in very impoverished conditions. As an adolescent he participated in street gangs, but after his marriage at the age of twenty he settled down, learned a trade (making britches), and opened a shop. He read voraciously; soon he was involved in political discussions and in the publishing of pamphlets. These activities led him to work with other radicals and become active in their issues, particularly the reform of Parliament and the beginnings of the union movement; he led one of the first strikes in his trade.

Among this generally like-minded group, Place was unique in introducing family planning and promoting dissemination of physiological and birth control information as an important activity of the radical movement. He and his wife had fifteen children and he could note the effect of continuous childbearing on his wife's health and on the economic hardship of his family. He also felt keenly from his own experience the lack of elementary knowledge of the physiology of sex among great masses of people.

General knowledge of the physiology of human reproduction at the time was in the most rudimentary stages. Some manuals were available that gave some elementary information; one of the most popular was called *Aristotle's Compleat Masterpiece: in three parts: displaying the secrets of nature and the generation of man.* It was used as a combined sex guide and obstetric manual by professionals and lay public alike and was consulted from the eighteenth to the beginning of the twentieth century. Place (1972) describes his embarrassing experience in school when he was called on to expound the first chapter of Matthew (the conception and birth of Jesus) and was unable to apply his knowledge gained from the manual to the description of Mary's conception and pregnancy and the birth of Jesus. This experience made him aware of the need for manuals that could be generally understood. It also foreshadowed the challenge to the Gospels implicit in the knowledge of actual reproductive physiology, which led, at least for Place and his friends, to atheism. This implication gave the movement in its beginnings an additional obstacle.

In his political activities, Place came into close contact with the leading thinkers of his day, especially those with advanced radical ideas. As Place discovered, the question of population control and family planning did not fit easily into the general political division between radicals and conservatives. The former wanted to give more economic and political power to the working classes through social legislation, power of trade unions, and reform of the electoral process, while conservatives tried to keep this power in the hands of the few and relied on market forces to counteract social ills. Concern with population problems, then as now, was not necessarily radical or conservative. In fact, Malthus himself had raised the threat of overpopulation as a conservative argument against the radical Godwin. On the other hand, one of Place's prominent radical colleagues, William Cobbett, was an outspoken opponent of Malthus's population principles.

Place's position in the ensuing controversy showed the different directions family planning policies could take. Unlike other protagonists, he had a strong incentive to support family planning from his own experience. He had been married early, before he was twenty, and he credited his wife's influence for the stability and purpose that his life had from then on. This alone would have made him oppose Malthus's prescription of delayed marriage. His early experience with London low life made him doubt even more the practicality of delayed marriage as a remedy for the poor. He testified that without the stability of married life he would have likely become a professional criminal, and he saw therefore social benefits from early marriage of the poor. Further, because of their fifteen children he could attest to the toll that marital fertility exacted from both parents. Place accepted Malthus's principles, namely the unfavorable effects of population increase, but found the means he advocated, late marriage and abstinence, to be extremely unrealistic, even detrimental. From his point of view, contraception was far more practical, and he introduced a procontraception position into the radical movement, combining population control with the idea of family planning for the first time.

Place published pamphlets and broadsides on many topics of the day, but his most important book dealt with population control. The immediate occasion for Place's publication was Godwin's delayed answer to Malthus. Godwin's book, *On Population* (1820), was published more than twenty years after the first edition of Malthus's treatise; it reasserted the optimistic point of view that subsistence could be improved while population increase was accommodated. Today most people agree that this was one of Godwin's weaker books, but at the time his reputation was so great that the book made an impression simply as the great man's answer to Malthus. Place took it upon himself to write a lengthy defense of Malthus, *Illustrations and Proofs of the Principle of Population* (1822). A great part of his discussion was a technical demographic argument, for instance, which country should be taken as the model for unrestrained population increase. This part mainly refined and justified Malthus's theory. In one chapter, however, Place went beyond Malthus and contradicted him.

Here he brought family planning into the discussion of population economics. Citing his own experience, he advocated early marriage and prevention of conception within marriage. This chapter of his book was the first public advocacy of birth control as a remedy to the population problem, an idea that eventually transformed an academic discussion into a social movement. By an ironic twist, Place's ideas came to be called not Placeism, but neo-Malthusianism.

Given the atmosphere of the times, Place was circumspect in presenting his new ideas. He is not specific in his book about the means of contraception, nor does he advocate any concerted program to promote it. Cautiously, he advocates economic changes that would provide strong motivation for small families, including freedom of business formation, free foreign trade, and freedom of association of workers, i.e., trade unions. (In this last item he contradicts the ideas of his economic mentors, Adam Smith and Thomas Malthus). Place's role in starting the family planning movement lies in his linking economic progress to family planning within marriage, even if he did not show specifically how family planning could be accomplished. But he introduced a new topic for discussion and presented a new agenda for the advocates of change.

Reproductive Physiology

The new possibility of individual family planning shown in Place's work advanced quickly to specifics. Place promoted more information by collaborating on a series of pamphlets that were commonly known as the "Diabolical handbills." Place himself stayed anonymous, and he secured the cooperation of Richard Carlile. Carlile was more of an agitator; he had been jailed for union activity and for blasphemy, but he had used his imprisonment to assemble a group of loyal followers. His greater willingness to take risks complemented Place's more intellectual approach.

Place set up Carlile in a print shop to publish their handbills, as well as other radical classics. The shop produced the most explicit advocacy of contraception to date *Every Woman's Book* (1826).

Place and Carlile's collaboration established family planning as an item on the radical agenda. Although not accepted by all, family planning could now be discussed within this circle. New publications aided the dissemination of these ideas on both sides of the Atlantic. Robert Dale Owen's *Moral Physiology* (1830) and George Drysdale's *Elements of Social Science* (1859) were the most successful; Owen's father, Robert Owen, had been a utopian social reformer and moved to the United States, where he founded the colony of New Harmony, Indiana. Robert Dale Owen continued his father's work, especially on sexual relations and introduced Carlile's work in America. Here it caught the attention of Dr. Charles Knowlton, who wrote his own book *The Fruits of Philosophy: An Essay on the Population Question* (Chandrasekar 1981) in 1832. Knowlton's work happened to have a greater influence in Britain, where it became the center of the first publicized opposition, than in its native country. The story of the fight this book engendered serves to introduce some of the flamboyant personalities characteristic of the early history of the movement.

Charles Knowlton

Knowlton himself had a comparatively quiet life. A physician of Ashfield, Massachusetts, he also had wide interests on philosophical and social topics and published a book proposing a completely materialistic doctrine of human life and action. In his practice he came to realize the extent of ignorance of reproduction among his patients, and he became conscious of the dangers of unrestricted fertility, on both the social and the personal level. He first prepared a set of notes on reproduction and contraception for his patients and, encouraged by their reception, arranged for the publication of his book. As he was a physician, his book had the ring of authority and gave more thorough information than had been possible for the previous pamphleteers. In fact, it was the first medical discussion of contraception in the 1700 years since Galen. The book treated in four chapters totaling fifty pages the desirability of limitation of family size, reproduction ("generation"), planning and checking conception, and the nature of the reproductive instinct (Chandrasekar 1981).

The legality of books dealing with the physiology of sexual behavior had long been questionable, both in England and in the United States.

Knowlton published his book in 1832; in the same year he was fined fifty dollars and costs and convicted to three months of hard labor. Two years later he was brought into court again, but the case was dismissed. In spite of this experience and the success of his book, Knowlton returned to private practice and a quiet life; little is known of his further career until his death in 1850.

Knowlton's part in the birth control movement is due more to the fate of his book after his death than to his personal efforts while alive. The book was hugely successful and was published in England one year after its original publication in the United States. Without any further legal trouble it went through nine editions and sold forty thousand copies in forty years. When the original publishers died, another publisher, Henry Watts, bought the copyright and brought out a new illustrated edition in 1877. At that time, more than a quarter century after Knowlton's death, his book became the focus of a new social development.

The situation in England had changed from Place's time. By the middle of the century the economic dislocation that provided the main impetus for the radical movement had subsided, but by the late 1870s the economy went into a prolonged slump and economic questions came to the fore again. Concern about the capacity of the country to absorb the increasing population, which had been assumed during the period of increasing prosperity, rekindled interest and reignited the controversy surrounding family planning. Even a Malthusian League was formed in 1861, but it did not achieve much success. New questions also gained prominence, particularly concerning position of women, a problem considered by such writers as George Eliot, and such philosophers as John Stuart Mill.

The new intellectual climate encouraged reformers to settle the question of the legitimacy of publication of contraception manuals. Knowlton's book, in the new illustrated edition, provided a case in point. Those in favor of legal publication found an advocate in one of the remarkable women of the time.

The Bradlaugh-Besant Trial

Annie Besant (1847–1933) was one of those people whose experience ranged through the whole society of her time; her life intersected with many politically and intellectually prominent contemporaries (Besant 1893, Chandrasekar 1981, Dinnage 1986). She was examined for her degree in botany by Thomas Huxley; published a magazine that launched the career of George Bernard Shaw, she was one of the founders of the Fabian Society, the intellectual foundation of the British Labour Party; was the last English president of Indian National Congress until she was defeated by Mohandas Gandhi; and ended her life as the leader of the Theosophical movement founded by Madame Blavatsky, which owes much of its continuing influence to Besant's organizational effort. Theosophism, a mystical doctrine that espouses the transmigration of souls, is opposed to limitation of fertility, because bodies are seen as only temporary homes for ever reborn souls. Besant wrote a pamphlet, *Theosophy and the Law of Population,* in 1896, repudiating her advocacy of family planning. Although she devoted the remainder of her life to theosophy, she changed her mind again on population control in 1930, when she published a new pamphlet under the same title, combining theosophy with acceptance of Malthusian principles. The activity that concerns us here occurred in first third of her life (Chandrasekar 1981).

Besant had a strict religious upbringing and first envisaged a career as a missionary. Her marriage to an orthodox minister turned out to be ideologically and emotionally unworkable, and she started to break away from Christianity. The personal problems of the couple were aggravated by sexual ignorance and her insistence, against her husband's will, that they limit the number of children to two; the marriage was dissolved and Annie Besant resumed her education, principally in biological fields. Association with like-minded people completed her break with Christianity and her espousal of current radical ideas.

She soon published several pamphlets and books, among them *The Law of Population* (1877), which carried on the amalgamation of Malthus's, Place's, and Carlile's ideas, with added arguments derived from her medical studies. Although with the publication of this book she achieved prominence in the emerging family planning movement, her main impact came not from her own writing, but from her legal battles for freedom of publication.

For several years Besant worked on the *National Reformer,* a journal published by Charles Bradlaugh. Bradlaugh was active throughout his life in radical causes; he had married Carlile's daughter, an instance of the combination of personal and ideological involvement. Two of his special interests were birth control and freedom of the press. Both these interests came together in his cooperation with Annie Besant.

The issue of freedom of the press arose in connection with Knowlton's book. *The Fruits of Philosophy* had been published and sold without hindrance for decades. But, when Watts, who had obtained the copyright, let a Bristol printer, Henry Cook, print an illustrated edition, the book was found to be obscene, partly because of the illustrations, and Cook was convicted to two years' hard labor. When Watts tried to dissociate himself from this enterprise, Besant and Bradlaugh stepped in. With Watts's permission, they reissued the book, without the offending illustrations, but with a new introduction. In a conscious arrangement for a test case, Besant and Bradlaugh notified the relevant London offices and sent two copies to the prosecutor. They were promptly indicted and arranged for maximum publicity for the trial. The trial lasted five days, attracted twenty thousand people by some counts, and was widely reported in the press. This event marked the introduction of the family planning movement into public consciousness.

The ostensible defendants in the trial were Annie Besant and Charles Bradlaugh, but the actual focus of the arguments was public discussion of contraception. The prosecution called the volume "a dirty, filthy book" that no right-thinking Englishman would want in his house. The grounds for prosecution were unclear, however, which showed the ambiguous dividing line in the law between discussion of contraception and obscenity. The prosecution tried to imply that Malthusian arguments advocate and facilitate promiscuity, but the judge ruled that it was not a germane argument in the case. The defendants succeeded in airing their point of view. They impressed the court and the audience by their knowledge of the main issues, the need for small families, and the ambiguities of the obscenity statute. The judge in his summary favored the defendants: the jury found the book obscene while clearing the defendants of any immoral intent. When the defendants declared their intentions of keeping up publication of the book, the judge had no alternative but to find them guilty. On appeal, however, the judgment was reversed, because the prosecution had not indicated which specific passages of the book were obscene. This looks like a technicality, but it shows the difficulty of pinpointing what actually is obscene in a discussion of contraception.

The principal effect of the trial was exactly what Besant and Bradlaugh had wanted. Contraception was treated in the press, first in the reports of the trial, and then in the public discussion of the issues that followed. Contraception became a public issue, even a political one, and was crucial in several election districts in the next election. The trial precipitated the emergence of an organized movement. The Malthusian League was revived in 1877 (Ledbetter 1976) and became the focus of the movement in England for about fifty years. In a real sense, the action of the few people brought about the origin of the birth control movement in England, and in the United States as well.

The U.S. Background

While the family planning movement was launched in England as part of a general reevaluation of social conditions, the situation was different in the United States. The ideas of the English radical movement had spread, but the context was different. For example, the name of the English liberal party in the early part of the nineteenth century, Whigs, was the name of the conservative party in the United States. The revolution in which the country was founded was in some ways a forerunner of the French Revolution, and the feudal and mercantile conditions that the radicals opposed in England as well were similar to those that provoked the American Revolutionary War. Both the connections and the differences between England and the United States became important in the rise of the family planning movement in the latter country.

We have noted previously the easy exchange of persons and ideas between the two countries. The Besant-Bradlaugh trial centered around a book that was written and widely used in the United States. In turn, some English radical leaders found it possible to use the undeveloped areas of the United States for their social experiments. Robert Owen founded a colony in New Harmony, Indiana, whose novel tenets included the use of birth control. His son introduced Carlile's work in the country and was a mentor of Bradlaugh (Harrison 1969). In fact, many of the utopian communities that sprang up on the frontier introduced a variety of forms of sexual relations that were in effect means of population control. They may have had some influence in laying the groundwork for acceptance of family planning.

Several unique characteristics of the United States influenced the development of the population movement. One of them was the demographic situation. Malthus had used the United States as the model of a country where maximum increase of human population was possible. One of the main tasks of the nation, as its leaders and thinkers saw it, was the settlement of the West, which required not only the increase of the native population, but immigrants as well—and the absorption of immigrants raised its own issue. Finally, the main political problem in the early part of the century was slavery, a major national concern. These three problems, Western settlement, development and absorption of immigrants, and slavery, moved American public debate in a special direction.

Medicine and Religion

Another important characteristic of the country derived from its middle-class culture, namely, the importance of the medical profession (Starr 1982). In the highly stratified and aristocratic society of Europe, medicine and the other professions were part of a lower rung of society, the middle classes, and only gradually acquired a respected status. In the comparative absence of aristocracy in the United States, professionals started out with an advantage because of their specialized and needed knowledge, and they organized quickly to maintain and expand their privileged position. Because of the power of the profession, therefore, the question of birth control became largely a medical problem. While the books about birth control written in England were mainly by laymen, Place, Carlile, Besant, the crucial medical book was imported from the United States. As a medical book, Knowlton's was more likely to be read and accepted in society than the "diabolical handbills" in Francis Place's tradition.

The initial hurdle that the American movement had to overcome was its relation to the medical profession. Contraceptive instruction and distribution was considered to be a purely medical function; lay people could not interfere with medical autonomy. But the physicians themselves showed little interest in these topics. The movement therefore had to work on alternative paths: letting lay people do some of the work, making all the medical activities connected with family planning important parts of the medical profession, and making family planning part of public policy.

Another circumstance of American history influenced the origin of the family planning movement. In England the radical movement was often linked to resistance to the established, Anglican church. Leadership in social change was often assumed by the members of the dissenting, non-Anglican, churches and by freethinkers. The United States, however, had no established church and the Episcopalian church, which corresponds to the Church of England, exerted power in only a few states. The dissenting groups, some of whom had left England just to escape Anglican domination, became dominant in many parts of the country and they, in turn, proceeded to set the social standards. The puritan influence of the dissenters included opposition to alcohol, pornography, prostitution, and unconventional sexual behavior; it tended in the long run to include opposition to birth control practices as well. Thus, the original opposition to the teaching of contraception came from the popular moralists, not from the institutions of the religious establishment.

Since there were no dissenting religious groups advocating contraception, in contrast to England, the dissemination of birth control information stayed mainly a professional matter within medicine during this period. The early part of the nineteenth century saw few popular reformers like Place and Carlile who tried to reach the general public on their own. The work of radical thinkers exhausted itself in the abolition movement. After the legal abolition of slavery some of this effort, at least in New England, was transferred in part to women's rights. (Henry James's novel, *The Bostonians*, shows this development). But even here the emphasis was not on birth control, but on other aspects of women's emancipation. After the losses of young men in the Civil War the need for family size reduction was not immediately apparent. Western expanded settlement, which was enhanced by Civil War legislation, and the rise of industry made neonatalist policy, increasing the birth rate, not implausible. There was no demographic pressure for population control and contraception was controlled quietly by the medical profession.

The climate for family planning was therefore quite unfavorable for a long time. The puritan, moralistic heritage created even more opposition to public discussion of the issue than in Victorian England or in European countries. Puritanism, of course, did not inhibit widespread concern with sexual matters and even may have promoted their diffusion into unrelated matters (Foucault 1980, Gay 1984), but it did encourage barriers to the free discussion that is necessary for coordinated social action. The demographic situation made discussion of the economic problems of overpopulation unlikely and eliminated this avenue to concern with family planning. Finally, the medical profession may have promoted the actual use of contraception, but only on a one-to-one basis (Luker 1984).

The Comstock Act

The social situation was reflected in the passage of the Comstock Act in 1872. Anthony Comstock (1844–1915) was a religious and moral crusader who was especially concerned with the fight against commercialized prostitution and pornography. He succeeded in getting the law passed that bears his name, an act forbidding the use of the mail for obscene materials. Almost at the last minute contraception was included under the definition of obscene, and it is not clear whether all congressmen voting on the act knew clearly its extent (Reed 1978). Comstock himself was extremely satisfied with this definition. He became very active in enforcing the law, even going so far as to entrap physicians into ordering material declared obscene by the act. In addition, state laws suppressing obscenity were enacted, which inhibited within-state distribution of contraception. To coordinate and enhance his efforts, Comstock helped to found the Society for the Suppression of Vice, which stayed in the forefront of this struggle. The name of the society probably helped form the association in the popular mind between the terms *contraception* and *vice*.

The act reinforced the special position of the medical profession as the only source of contraception. Neither the Comstock Act itself nor the subsequent state acts prohibited the use of contraception or its medical prescription. Some state acts, however, prohibited giving advice on the topic, while allowing prescription on demand, a difference not always easy to enforce in practice. These acts tried to define a role for the physician as healer, but not as teacher. This formulation excluded even further people who were only teachers or nonmedical helpers of other kinds and reinforced the exclusion of the lay public from family planning.

The codification of the puritan attitude into statute law had its dangers for both sides of the issue. It did make dissemination of much material dangerous and difficult, but the laws also provided a target for the opponents of puritanism. And later, when this period of social unrest did produce leaders for many causes, including family planning, they found a well-defined issue to engage in.

Urban Radicals and Anarchists

The last decades of the century produced social unrest in the United States similar to that in England. In part it was a consequence of the same conditions, economic depression with interruption of social mobility, realization of bad labor conditions, and the rise of new ideologies that were adapted to the changed conditions of the modern age. To this were added some conditions peculiar to the United States. Large numbers of immigrants who had been peasants and wanted to build farms of their own had no funds beyond their passage or railroad tickets and had to stay in coastal or railhead cities where they formed large ethnic enclaves (Handlin 1951).

The rise of a new radical movement was furthered by the poor conditions in the cities, and leadership came from the immigrant communities themselves. New ideologies had been common among some of these groups in their countries of origin and they discussed them in their new location. A radical leadership arose that gave a particular flavor to the politics of this period. The diverse socialist, Marxist, and anarchist groups never reached a strength sufficient to truly affect the social and political history of the country in the twentieth century; social scientists still discuss the question of why no radical or socialist working-class movement has lasted in the United States. During this period, however, several very active people and groups left their mark on the development of a number of policy issues, including family planning.

Emma Goldman

The radical leader most involved in promoting family planning was Emma Goldman (1869–1940). She was born in Russia and came to the United States in 1886 (Goldman 1931, Drinnon 1961). Working in sweatshops in New York and Rochester she did not find the opportunities that she had expected and soon became involved in anarchist movements. An unfortunate marriage to a naturalized American lasted only a year, but it gave her U.S. citizenship. She returned to New York where she became a prominent speaker in the anarchist cause. At this time she started her lifelong involvement with Alexander Berkman, another anarchist leader. Berkman attempted to assassinate Henry Frick, the president of the Carnegie Steel Corporation and was sentenced to twenty-one years in a penitentiary. The whole affair split the anarchists and left Goldman as their most visible leader. Within a year she was arrested for inciting to riot and jailed for a year. During her imprisonment she received some training as a nurse, and she was so impressed by nursing's relevance to the problems of the poor that she returned to Europe and took a year's training in nursing and midwifery at the *Allgemeines Krankenhaus* in Vienna.

Emma Goldman is the closest American parallel to the English radicals for whom the birth control movement was only a part of a general struggle for a fundamental change in society; her influence on radical political ideas supplemented her work in family planning. On her return from Europe she worked in slum areas and got more and more interested in medical and pregnancy problems. She obtained financial support from individual sponsors and returned to Europe to study medicine. Once there, however, she devoted her time mainly to political activity and her sponsors withdrew their support. On her way back to the United States she attended a neo-Malthusian congress. She collected there a number of pamphlets and other publications and returned in December 1900 ready to combine anarchist and family planning activities.

A few months after her return, however, the assassination of President William McKinley by an anarchist ushered in a period of government action against anarchism. Goldman became the main public symbol of anarchism—the next decade was the one of her greatest prominence—and was also a target of official action.

During this period she founded a magazine, *Mother Earth,* to increase the impact of her ideas. She also entered into a long relationship with Ben L. Reitman (1879–1942). Reitman was a street kid who had found some sponsors to help him complete a medical degree. His sympathies remained with his poor background, however, and he often tried to assume the role of "king of the hoboes," generally playing a frivolous role among the earnest anarchists. He did, however, lend his medical background and interests to the cause. Officially he was Goldman's manager, securing meeting halls and arranging for the distribution of pamphlets that gave medical information on birth control techniques.

Goldman, Reitman, and their associates succeeded in keeping their ideas salient by conducting mass meetings, pushing the limits of legality and challenging the authorities. In 1910 *Mother Earth* was confiscated by Comstock in his role as a postal inspector giving the anarchists an opportunity to expose him to ridicule. In this case other postal inspectors found nothing objectionable in the issue and released the magazine. This and similar events gave Goldman some support among people who objected to her politically radical ideas. With the coming entry of the United States into World War I the combination of the issues that the anarchists advocated—anti–involuntary pregnancy, antimarriage, anticonscription, antiwar—became too much to escape prosecution. In 1916 Goldman and Reitman were arrested at a New York meeting for a talk similar to many that she had given all over the country; they were sentenced to a short prison term.

The next years were taken up by national and international events, the World War and the Russian Revolution. Goldman and Berkman (who had been released from prison in 1906) were acquitted in a conspiracy trial in 1916, but were deported in a mass action against undesirable aliens in 1919. Goldman's citizenship was revoked in a controversial proceeding on the grounds that her husband had obtained his citizenship illegally. Goldman went to Russia, but was disappointed in the outcome of the revolution and left Russia for Western Europe and finally Canada. Her general prominence and especially her place in the birth control movement faded. Reitman returned to Chicago and worked on skid row on welfare and the control of social diseases.

The radical, anarchist wing of the family planning movement ended in failure just as the whole anarchist movement did. The reasons for this failure seem to be that Americans are generally hostile to class political movements and that the Democratic and Republican party organizations that had absorbed the urban poor were efficient. In the promotion of contraception Goldman and Reitman had some success. While how much information they distributed and how effective it was cannot be measured, it was the most reliable information available for the public at the time. The brushes with governmental authorities gave the issue much publicity and secured some important allies; the actions of the anarchist leaders made later attacks on the Comstock Act much easier.

The importance of the anarchists lay not only in their immediate impact, but also in the lessons they taught the movement. They demonstrated the danger of bringing contraception into too close an alliance with other issues. In this case one cannot talk even of a *family* planning movement, as the leaders were antifamily in general; this position damaged their efforts as atheism had hurt the movement in England. The main issue, however, is simply that a movement rooted in extreme splinter groups had little chance to gain sufficient influence to produce social change. The emergence of a successful family planning movement depended on two developments: the large-scale recognition of a need for population control and the efforts of individual families and individuals to limit fertility. Both lines required the acceptance of new ideas, new techniques, and new attitudes. In modern Western society legitimation of a movement of this kind comes when movement leaders ally with professionals in the field. In the family planning movement these alliances were of crucial importance.

Chapter Four

Leaders and Organization

By the end of the nineteenth century many factors set the stage for the acceptance of the idea of family planning. For one thing, it was no longer either morally or technically unthinkable. The aims of population control were now discussed within the framework of political economy. On the family and individual level, many reformers expressed concerns about family size and the associated hardship on women. Effective means for contraception became more widely known; distribution of instructional pamphlets and books became a public issue. The attempts of suppression and resulting police and court struggles had themselves brought the issue of family planning to public attention.

Like various other scientific innovations, family planning accompanied a change in basic features of the society. Physicians and reformers of the nineteenth century had introduced the topic into the public domain for the first time. Additional effort was required to transform it in the twentieth century into a positive social ideal.

For a social movement to be effective, it needs its own individual tradition. It must identify a core of people who are devoted to its aims, including a few outstanding persons who will be seen as heroes, heroines, or martyrs. It must have a picture of its opposition, preferably personified, and a history of its own struggles, defeats, and eventual triumphs. In short, it needs a mythology, a vivid history of its past as a source of strength and distinction. In the family planning movement one can discern the development of the essential features of a heroic myth in the half century since the events, in particular the identification of leaders who devoted their lives to the cause, who suddenly felt a call for their mission in life, whose lives were extraordinary in success, failure, and hardship, and who performed great deeds and underwent great risks to put the movement on the map. Their lives are well known, but mainly in terms of their inspirational function in the movement. The protagonists in this early movement are seen by the later followers as larger than life (Back 1988).

Even quite recent biographies of the founders see their lives as enveloped in some mystery; further investigation shows that this mystery was purposely introduced, mainly by the founders themselves. Apparently one of the qualities needed to start a social movement is just this capacity to establish a mythical stature for oneself. Part of this quality is a strong involvement in the issues, which entails taking small events in the movement (as well as related events in one's own life) with the utmost seriousness. Thus early leaders in social movements often show not only idealism, devotion, and hard work, but also high degrees of pettiness and a tendency toward merciless infighting.

The important legacy of these heroes and heroines is the establishment of a permanent organization, which assures permanence to the movement. The excitement of the early struggle cannot be maintained indefinitely; the permanent structure of an organization with officers, dues, and assigned functions can maintain efforts when the original personal enthusiasm of individual leaders and devoted followers is gone. Sociologists speak of this change as the routinization of charisma or the change from a nascent to an institutional state (Alberoni 1984).

Family planning has so many aspects that the movement could have gone in several directions. It could have been dominated by the large-scale concerns of the political economists; it could have been a revolutionary movement allied with the anarchists; it could have purely medical advance; or it could been an expression of sexual morality. The extent to which each of these aspects dominated was in great part due to the personal predilections of the founders and thus the story of this "heroic" period is an important part of movement history.

The role of individuals in the history of social movements has long been a controversial topic. On one extreme one can say that some appropriate social change would have been necessary in any case and the efforts of particular persons made little difference. On the other extreme one can claim that movement history reflects primarily the actions of great heroes and heroines. In general, it is clear that some phases of a movement need the presence of strong individuals who will undertake the difficult actions required and make appropriate choices at critical junctures. These heroic figures, if successful, combine response to the needs of the movement at the particular time with sensitivity to the needs of possible audiences. The initial phase of a movement, when its ideas are crystallizing, but when these ideas are still opposed by the principal values of the society, is called the "heroic" period. In the family planning movement heroic figures arose who concentrated the movement's aims to a struggle for availability of contraception. They also led it to a special relation with the medical profession and to a position in society from which it could successfully promote its aims.

The actions of the heroic founders of the family planning movement led to its transformation into a middle-class cause, which was respectable and achieved its influence through convention channels. This transformation occurred partly against the inclination of the leaders themselves who had started out in a radical working-class atmosphere. They showed their acceptance of the needs of the movement over personal predilections, a flexibility that made them successful in promoting the movement's aims.

Margaret Sanger

The identity of the movement in the early twentieth century could only be established through severing connections with former radical allies. This led to personal and organizational conflicts and some of the available sources graphically express the emotions generated by the struggle. The main actors reflected these conflicts on a personal level in their careers, perhaps none more so than Margaret Sanger (Sanger 1938, Lader 1955, Kennedy 1970, Reed 1978, Douglas 1979). She does so because her career spans all phases of the movement such that other figures are often seen in relation to her; in addition she felt the opportunity and burden of her central position herself and contributed to the almost mythical role that she has assumed. Her self-presentation is therefore almost as important as the literal truth of her life.

Margaret Sanger (1879–1966) is generally known as the founder of the American birth control movement. In her early career she was involved with the working-class anarchists who had first taken up the fight for contraception; later she concentrated on developing a complicated relationship with the medical profession, gradually obtaining middle-class support. She lived long enough to see family planning become a respectable institution and her own elevation as an almost mythical figure of international renown.

She was born Margaret Higgins in Corning, New York, the daughter of an Irish-American stonecutter, who devoted his life to the active dissemination of freethinking ideals and ideas of radical economic and political change. He transmitted his values and his outspokenness to his children. Margaret was training as a nurse, but at the age of nineteen she married an artist, William Sanger, and spent the next few years as a suburban housewife. The family moved to New York and intellectual and rebellious attitudes reawakened. She soon found contact with those who made up labor, anarchist, and revolutionary circles, such as Emma Goldman and her friends; Mabel Dodge, whose salon was the center of the revolutionary movement; and William Haywood, the labor leader with whom Sanger had a long association. Within all this ferment Sanger maintained her own interests and her own direction.

She also started to work in nursing, partly to help family finances. In 1912, during the course of her work, she had an experience, which, according to her, determined her future life. She was called to attend a Mrs. Sadie Sachs who was gravely ill following a self-induced abortion. Her physician acknowledged that any further pregnancy could endanger her life; but the only advice he could give was: "Tell Mr. Sachs to sleep on the roof." (This has become a fighting slogan in the family planning movement.) Later that year Mrs. Sachs died after trying to end another unwanted pregnancy. Margaret Sanger describes how she wandered all night through the city, thinking of all the households in misery and of all the women suffering and dying for lack of knowledge and counsel. When dawn arrived she had found new strength and a direction for her life's work. This story, at least in the version in which it has come down to us, may be apocryphal, but it corresponds to the sudden insights and conversions that often occur to leaders and founders of social movements. It is clear that she was concerned with improvement in social welfare and closely connected with people who wanted radical social change. An experience such as the one with Mrs. Sachs crystallized her ideas, after which she drew on her training and skills and began to pursue her own goals in conjunction with her friends.

Within a year she decided that insufficient material on birth control was available in the United States, while improved methods were known in Europe. Even written material describing these advances was difficult to obtain in the United States because of the Comstock Act. Further, training in contraceptive techniques was offered for paramedical personnel by some centers in Europe, such as the Malthusian League in London. Haywood suggested therefore that she go to Europe where he could give her the necessary introduction. The Sangers' marriage had been failing for a time and the trip to Europe became a way to make a break. They left together for Europe in the fall of 1913 and Margaret returned to the United States in December alone.

On her return she founded and edited a magazine called *The Woman Rebel*. This magazine remained within an anarchist-radical framework, proclaiming on its masthead opposition to all domination, including sexual: "No God, No Masters." Her correspondence with her husband at the time shows that these questions were not purely ideological, but represented personal concerns.

Her friends William Haywood and Emma Goldman were among the contributors to the journal, but Sanger herself was the mainstay of the paper and contributed much material advocating contraception. One of the enduring contributions of the journal was the introduction of the term *family planning*. She soon ran afoul of the Comstock Act. One early issue was seized by the Post Office, but, as in the Bradlaugh-Besant case, the government could not identify the specific passages that were objectionable.

Unlike the published material involved in the earlier case, Sanger's paper had really very little actual description and instruction on contraception, mainly appealing to women to keep their family size small without telling them how. But the fight with the Post Office continued and Margaret Sanger was finally called to court. Here the stories differ. Her own account claims that she had hardly any advance notice to prepare her defense, while it seems from other sources that she was accorded all the normal privileges of due process. It soon became apparent that she was running the risk of going to prison and she decided to leave the country. She went first to Montreal and sailed in October 1914 to Europe. On this trip her main contacts were people involved in family planning, especially medical, while her interest in other issues, such as anarchism, started to wane. The period of this stay in England, 1914–1916, marks her emergence as a fully-fledged leader in family planning.

Sanger in England

The story of birth control in England forms an interesting contrast and complement to the origins of the American movement. The history of the early English movement is dominated by the legacy of Malthus; the economic, demographic side of the argument prevailed in England for a long time. The importance of population control for the society was stressed. An organized movement emphasizing these issues had started earlier than in the United States. The founding of the main organization, the Malthusian League, in 1877 was mainly due to Charles Bradlaugh and Annie Besant. The publicity surrounding their trial gave impetus to the league; it became a small, but active discussion group, which tried to produce educational material for the working classes (Ledbetter 1976). But in contrast to American family planning ideology, which was originally working class–oriented, the English ideology followed Malthus's economic theories, which exalted free competition and individualism and advocated birth control in part because it would prevent unrest among the working classes. In this posture the league had enemies from two sides: they were attacked for discussing taboo topics and at the same time were pictured by Marxist and other socialists as defenders of the status quo, even at the cost of working people's lives. The league concentrated therefore on continuing their early work in producing sex education material and some of their writers and publishers continued to have troubles with courts.

Both Bradlaugh and Besant gradually dropped out of the leadership of the league. Their drift away from family planning demonstrates the different strains of the movement. Bradlaugh started work in politics and was elected to Parliament; his strongest concern was with free thought (he refused to take the oath of office on the Bible) and he toned down the forbidden discussion of sex, especially since a few years earlier, in 1876, Viscount Amberley (Bertrand Russell's father) had been defeated for election because of a public lecture in favor of neo-Malthusianism. Besant became more attracted to socialism and gradually lost her enthusiasm for the Malthusian cause; her later work for Indian independence and theosophy changed her point of view completely. The fate of these founders shows the narrow appeal of the birth control movement at this time; it could not even keep the interest of its leaders.

The leadership of the movement fell to the physician Charles Robert Drysdale, his wife, Alicia Vickery Drysdale, and their family (Reed 1978). Drysdale's principal effort was directed toward disseminating information on sexuality, following the tradition of Knowlton and others. All the Drysdales published copiously, volumes on all aspects of sexual questions (even before their involvement with the Malthusian League) and instructional pamphlets for the Malthusian League. Charles Robert himself was cautious in other respects, publishing articles in controversial journals only under his initials or a pseudonym. Under the Drysdales' leadership the league became a source for medical information and some training and their writings became principal sources of birth control information, in England as well as in the United States (Drysdale 1857). Nevertheless, the league had little direct influence on the section of the population to which its efforts were directed, as their economic politics separated them from working-class movements.

Introduction to the work of the Malthusian League drew Margaret Sanger's interests away from radical social change to work on the medical aspects of contraception. At the league she obtained the best current information on birth control and even obtained some practical clinical training. Although she could not take the intensive course in contraceptive techniques offered in the league, because of her lack of professional background, she was allowed to take classes for nurses and midwifes.

Even more important for her personal and professional development was her association with Havelock Ellis (Ellis 1939, Grosskurth 1951). When they met, Ellis (1859–1939) was already established as a leading expert on sexual behavior and an advocate of sexual freedom. He had not been closely associated with any of the leading organizations, but at the end of the nineteenth century he had directed a "Fellowship of the New Life," which encouraged metaphysical, social, and interpersonal regeneration. He was a prolific and controversial author, and his works are still classics of anthropological and medical investigation of sexual behavior. His own personal life followed his rules for free sexual behavior, and it so happened that both he and Sanger were receptive to a new strong personal involvement at the time they met. Ellis guided Sanger's research in the European work on contraception. He advised her not to fight the American situation by defying the laws, but by showing the unreasonableness of the Comstock Act and working for its repeal. He helped her in planning her studies and travels to become an expert on the topic. In particular he introduced her to the work on contraception in Holland. There she met Dr. Johannes Rutgers who introduced her to a superior type of diaphragm. He also convinced her that effective birth control devices needed medical supervision in their introduction, contrary to her previous belief, advocated in her writings, that only women could help women. This conversion to the medical point of view became important in Sanger's later work.

Sanger and Ellis were also drawn into a passionate love affair. Their love changed later into close friendship and they continued a voluminous correspondence until the end of Ellis's life. Sanger's European stay took on the character of an apprenticeship. Ellis's influence on her directed the future course of her life. This influence was crucial not only for her, but for the history of the birth control movement. Apprenticeship abroad is a common event in the life of a typical movement hero or heroine.

Margaret Sanger returned to the United States in 1916. She was no longer a fugitive from justice, as the government had dropped the old charges. But she immediately had to face new public controversy. She had left a pamphlet, *Family Limitation,* to be printed in her absence and William Sanger, who was still technically married to Margaret, had to serve thirty days in prison. Thus, on her return Margaret Sanger was greeted with newspaper headlines linking her and birth control, and she appeared as the leading figure on this issue.

At this point all circumstances cooperated to launch her into a new career of leadership. The apprenticeship years had passed; she had acquired superior knowledge; she had lost some of the interest in her other political activities; she had asserted emotional freedom from her previous relationships: in short, she had become a new woman, personally as well as socially, and was ready to start a new life as a leader of a new movement.

The Birth of the Organized Movement

Sanger's new role also made her see that new action was necessary. To introduce birth control where it was needed, she had to do more than write and distribute information. This had been the weakness of the Malthusian League. Sanger was ready to start a clinic herself; a great part of her life in the next decades was devoted to combining her organizational work with medical and clinical experiences. She still had brushes with the law, but these were related to the legitimacy of her work on birth control clinics, not to abstract questions of civil liberties.

One of the advantages of the new orientation was the increasing autonomy of the family planning movement from other movements for social change. Contraception became less tied to specific political ideologies; it no longer suffered by being connected in the popular mind with anarchism, revolution, or with traditional economic theories. This made it possible for Sanger's work to be seen only in terms of immediate consequences. Autonomy from political ideology was achieved through professional orientation, which, in turn, led to a dependence on medical authority, a relationship that has persisted to the profit and loss of the movement.

This orientation did not mean that Margaret Sanger and her followers gave up theoretical discussions and inspirational writing; her books during this period proclaimed hopes for a better future and, with her new emphasis, asserted that all kinds of social gains would result from widely practiced contraception and the new sexual ethic. But her concentration on practical work gave her a unique position in the field. Many potential competitors had to come to terms with her, as she had by far the greatest experience and the best data of anyone in the field.

To attain and keep her position in the movement, Margaret Sanger had to fight on several fronts. She had to get birth control accepted, legally and socially, and she had to make it safe, efficient, and affordable for the masses. Besides dealing with her natural opponents, she also had to make some accommodation with the medical profession, which could be friend or foe. In addition, she had to fight battles within the movement itself, which as it grew naturally separated into rival factions, which were divided by the sources of their membership, their tactics and priorities, and by personal ambitions and antagonisms. The two decades that followed Margaret Sanger's return from Europe saw her achievement of the role for which her apprentice years had prepared her; they also showed the complex struggles she underwent to become the movement's heroine.

Upon her return Sanger opened a birth control clinic in Brownsville, a poor neighborhood of Brooklyn. In doing so, she violated the law that prohibited the sale and distribution of contraceptive material. Within a few days she and her sister, who worked with her in the clinic, were arrested and charged. The trials, coming on the heels of William Sanger's trial and the commotion aroused by her return, created much excitement. Many people came to her defense, and this was the last time that the old names from her anarchist days—Emma Goldman, Berkman, and others—came out publicly for Sanger. She introduced in her defense some of the civil rights issues that became important later: namely that the law interfered with a woman's rights to take care of her own body and therefore contravened the Constitution. This argument introduced the controversial right to privacy. At this time the argument was rejected and she did not pursue it to the higher federal courts. Sanger hoped that many women would follow her into defying the law, in a movement of mass civil disobedience, but these hopes were not fulfilled. The headlines she gained were soon lost as war news received more attention. The United States entered World War I in April 1917. This event led Goldman and her circle to concentrate on pacifism and to drop work on contraception. For Sanger it had the opposite effect. Although she continued her clinic work, she began to consider other, political, ways to reach her goals.

For the movement to be successful, the removal of the legal barriers to contraception was essential. This could be accomplished in two ways, either by changing the laws or by continually breaking them, which would lead to court challenges and unenforceability. Sanger and her friends had taken the second approach without great success. Havelock Ellis had encouraged her to take the first approach. During these years some groups had formed that used lobbying activities to get the anticontraceptive laws repealed. These groups were started by upper middle-class women, who had success during this period in getting two constitutional amendments, the eighteenth (Prohibition), and the nineteenth (women's suffrage), ratified. The National Birth Control League, one such group, was formed in 1915 with the express purpose of lobbying against restrictive laws, especially in New York. It was led by Mary Ware Dennett (1872–1947) who had been active in the other campaigns, especially suffrage, and also in the Democratic party. Dennett herself had won a court case in 1915, in which a sex education pamphlet was exempted from restrictive laws, because it had no lascivious intent (Dennett 1926). During the next years Sanger and Dennett fought for the leadership of the birth control movement; however, by their common aims they were also forced into grudging cooperation. Sanger did emerge as the winner, at least in terms of her later reputation, but she was clearly influenced by the tactics and the sources of support of Dennett and her associates.

The history of this struggle is similar to that of internal struggles in other social movements, which include a maze of different organizations, appeals to various loyalties, conflicts, and issues that seemed tremendously important at the time but which pall at a distance. It must be remembered, however, that the infighting of the different wings of the movement was only one part of the activities. All participants also had to carry on the fight for the movement's goals, which were still under heavy attack. The period from World War I to the height of the New Deal was one of great excitement for the movement and the basis of its ultimate success. It included organizational struggles as well as activities that positioned the movement for acceptance in society. The interaction of the two processes represents the main dynamic of a social movement on the path to success.

Margaret Sanger would not join the National Birth Control League, but she formed her own parallel organization, the New York Birth Control League, with the help of a few friends. One of these, Frederic Blossom, founded a new journal, the *Birth Control Review,* which was the official mouthpiece of the league. Blossom was an associate from the old radical days, a former organizer of the IWW, Haywood's labor union. The *Review* was a less controversial journal than the *Woman Rebel;* it printed more factual and statistical articles, fewer propagandistic pieces, and, in spite of its name, no direct information about birth control. It also attracted a wider variety of contributors and so kept Sanger in contact with some of her rivals.

In general the New York League was more radical than the National Birth Control League and its successor, the Voluntary Parenthood League. There were also tactical differences in outlook. Dennett, building on the success of the suffrage movement, wanted to concentrate on the federal level, in particular the repeal of the applicable parts of the Comstock Act, while Sanger worked on the state level, especially in New York, though both organizations lobbied in Albany (Reed 1978). The two women disagreed on which legal changes to advocate; and the disagreement, while it seems to be a minor technical point, had important consequences for the future development of the movement. Dennett wanted simply the phrase "for prevention of conception" stricken from the prohibition of sale of medical devices, which would have made contraceptives generally available for prevention of disease. Sanger wanted the use of contraception open for any reason at all, but only under medical supervision. Here the influence of her training in Europe showed itself. In any event, bills reflecting both positions were defeated at that time; in fact, most of the changes desired by the movement came about through judicial, not legislative, action. The struggle showed, however, Sanger's growing reliance on the medical profession, which at the time was generally not receptive to her ideas. In the long run, this alliance became very helpful to her eventual success. The question of medical control is still vitally important today in the discussion of abortion.

During the years after Margaret Sanger's return from Europe the organizational struggle within the nascent movement started to determine its future course. Dennett and her organizations, the National Birth Control League and the Voluntary Parenthood League, wanted to concentrate on legislative action and refused even financial support to Sanger, who went beyond this aim. Sanger with her New York Birth Control League and its successor, the American Birth Control League, wanted to expand into other fields: judicial decisions, direct action, and generally wider ideological discussion, as shown in the *Birth Control Review.* In

1917 the journal underwent a crisis that was important in itself, but even more important for Sanger's future career.

Blossom, the journal's managing editor, quit in the spring of 1917, taking with him the journal's files, which included subscriber lists, account books, and funds, and anything else he could put his hands on. He jeopardized the survival of the journal, which was an important link in the movement. Sanger promptly went to the district attorney to seek redress. This action, which might seem like a natural recourse, marked a significant break in Sanger's relations with her old friends from the anarchist days. Using the machinery of the state to recover property—"property is theft" was the anarchist slogan—and especially inciting law enforcement agencies to attack a man of Blossom's credentials ran counter to the principles of the whole circle. Many of her old friends denounced Sanger for her action: this break acknowledged the new direction of the birth control movement, its beginning as a middle-class welfare movement. In this process Sanger came to accept Dennett's general stance, however much she wanted the movement to achieve its aims without Dennett.

Sanger's personal life during these years was conducive to success for her work. Her divorce became final in 1920; long before she had decided never to undergo again the restraints of domesticity and marriage. Her passionate affairs after this were mainly with men who were intellectually and dynamically her equals and who acknowledged her as such. Her partners were men who could help her, intellectually or practically, in her mission. We have seen how she combined love and discipleship in her relation with Havelock Ellis. The independent life of the "new woman" of the 1920s satisfied her emotionally, but she missed the stability, especially the financial stability, that marriage could give. She decided therefore to find a husband who could provide the practical help she needed. Although she probably did not go about it as coldbloodedly as is indicated in some of her writings, she succeeded in finding the arrangement she desired. She remarried to J. Noah H. Slee, a man twenty years her senior, who owned a drug company, and the Three-In-One Oil Company and had been a financial supporter of the movement. The marriage agreement stipulated that the two partners would maintain separate domiciles, not interfere with each other's business and private lives, and, if they were busy, maintain communication through their secretaries. This arrangement apparently remained satisfactory to both parents. Slee became the main benefactor of the American Birth Control League.

The combination of her earlier notoriety and her later personal and financial stability secured Margaret Sanger's position as the unifying symbol during the formative years of the movement. Her great strength continued to be her ability to catch popular attention. Her speeches attracted and provoked audiences. This notoriety accompanied the founding of the American Birth Control League in 1920. The founding was a climax of the First American Birth Control Conference, which she organized; the formation of the league, with Margaret Sanger as president, was announced at the final session, and competed quite successfully for headlines with major political events.

A few days later followed a meeting in New York's Town Hall where Sanger was scheduled to speak. A large detachment of police tried to prevent the meeting, and because of confusion in their orders they induced a large crowd action. People outside tried to get into the hall, people inside tried to get out, and in the midst of it all, Margaret Sanger, accompanied by a group of her followers and a police escort, was swept off to the police station. Soon it became clear that the police intervention had been instigated by the Catholic archdiocese and this, of course, became big news for the press. A substitute meeting was held a few days later in a different location, the city did not prosecute Sanger, and the whole affair helped to establish Margaret Sanger as the symbol of birth control. It also established the Catholic church as the preeminent foe of the movement, which had important consequences continuing to the present.

For a while the American Birth Control League was ruled almost dictatorially by Sanger, due to her undoubted prominence in the field, her control of the main financial support, and the personal magnetism she exerted upon many of the workers. In restrospect, it is surprising that she succeeded in holding on to her position as long as she did, considering that the league was so different from the organizations with which she had started. The membership consisted mainly of white, Protestant middle-class women, who endorsed the kind of middle-of-the-road politics that was almost anathema to the younger Sanger.

Sanger used her leadership position in the American movement to expand her activities in the international sphere. In the twenties she made several trips abroad and launched an international movement for family planning. She led the Sixth International Birth Control and Neo-Malthusian Conference in New York City in 1925. She had initial setbacks too, however. During 1926–27 she worked on organizing a World Population Conference, but when it met in Geneva in 1927, her place in the conference and the topic of birth control were entirely omitted. Her varying success was evidence of the conflict still existing between the purely demographic interests and the family planning activists. Cooperation would have been beneficial for the success of family planning, but only partial cooperation came much later.

An indirect consequence of Sanger's varied international activities was trouble at home. While she spent eighteen months in Europe to prepare for the World Population Conference, Ellen Dwight Jones, who was acting president of the American Birth Control League in Sanger's absence, tried to change the league's structure, removing it from Sanger's absolute control. The result was an ugly power struggle that Sanger eventually lost. First she resigned from the presidency, then Slee stopped his financial support, and then she severed all connection with the League. Jones and Sanger tried to divide the responsibilities so that Sanger would concentrate on the clinical aspect of birth control and the league on legislation. Sanger, however, did not quite keep to the agreement, founding new committees to promote legislation.

The organizational war lasted for years and Margaret never regained organizational power in the American movement she had founded. In the long run, this outcome may have been beneficial for both her and the movement. Margaret Sanger's position as a heroine was safe; she retained moral leadership of the worldwide movement and could concentrate on those actions that seemed most promising at different times. The league gradually developed an established pattern, with membership becoming respectable in many communities. The resulting attitude toward the movement was that it was a recognized alternative, a possible avenue for action, but it was still considered nonconformist. The next step, that of wide social acceptance, came from a different direction, namely the work of the demographers.

Chapter Five

The Road to Success

By the early 1930s an organized family planning movement had become a reality. In spite of many defeats family planning had become a reform issue to which committed followers devoted concerted efforts. Even the struggles between Margaret Sanger and her opponents indicated that control of the organization was important enough to fight for. The movement had become a middle-class civic enterprise, like advocacy of other reform issues at the time.

Yet the reform itself had still to be achieved; birth control itself had not become socially acceptable. For family planning to progress to that point, public beliefs of what was possible and practicable had to be changed. Before this could occur family planning activities had to be accepted as a consistent issue; as long as each new activity appeared as a discrete event, further progress was not possible. The task of the family planners from the 1930s onward was the elimination of negative sanctions. To achieve acceptance of family planning as a positive social effort required a new view, a normative change, in society's concern with population increase.

Margaret Sanger and Marie Stopes

Margaret Sanger insisted that the best way to establish family planning was by devotion to clinical progress. The more she was rebuffed politically by her own organization, the more she devoted her time to the medical side of the issue. In evaluating her work during the 1920s, one must keep in mind how much of her time and energy was devoted to this concern. As previously mentioned, she opened a clinic with her sister, and she persisted in her work at the clinic despite being prosecuted by police and the courts, and even spending a short time in jail.

She was partly inspired in this undertaking by a spirit of competition. The leader in the birth control movement in England was Marie Stopes (1880–1958), whose life in some ways paralleled Sanger's and in some contrasted with it (Stopes 1923, Maude 1924, Hall 1977, Soloway 1982). She was a pioneer in her concern and campaign against involuntary motherhood, but had reached this position primarily from the scientific, academic side. Her parents were progressive and interested in their daughter's education; like Margaret Sanger, she had contact with new ideas in her parents' home and was encouraged to continue her training. Here the paths of the two leaders diverged. Marie Stopes entered University College, London, where she had a brilliant career in several fields of biology. She continued her studies in Germany, at the University of Munich, where she obtained her doctorate. Soon after she obtained a lectureship in botany at the University of Manchester and gained an international reputation in her field, unusual for a woman at that time.

Marie Stopes had a whole range of interests beyond her scientific and academic work, but—again in contrast to Sanger—she was not actively involved in politics. Her work in family planning evolved mainly from personal experience. After a few months of marriage to a fellow biologist she felt that she was missing something from the union. From discussions with friends and some library research she learned the role sexual intercourse ought to play in a marriage for the satisfaction of the partners. She then realized that her husband was impotent, and the marriage was dissolved. This experience showed her vividly the widespread damage caused by lack of sexual knowledge; if even she, who had completed her dissertation on the reproductive system of a plant species, was so woefully ignorant, many young couples must surely need help. In characteristic fashion she started to remedy the situation by writing a book *Married Love* (1918), which has become a classic in the field of sex education. She was soon remarried to a wealthy businessman—in this her life paralleled Sanger's—and, with his financial help, started a family planning clinic in London.

Married Love included extremely graphic descriptions and English publishers refused to print it. Margaret Sanger helped find an American publisher for it and, after the book became a success in the United States, it was successfully published in England as well. But after this the relationship between the two women soured; Sanger resented Stopes's success and acclaim. Perhaps she felt Stopes had attained it too easily without serving an apprenticeship in work with the poor and radical politics. It also rankled her that Stopes's book as well as her clinic functioned successfully, that she was invited to many lectures without interference, in short that Marie Stopes had become the leading spirit of the family planning movement, a position Sanger had fought so dearly to achieve. Furthermore, the underlying ideology of the two women was really very different. Marie Stopes was politically conservative throughout her career; much of her interest in birth control was motivated by eugenic considerations. Thus she naturally drifted to cooperation with Sanger's organizational opponents, in particular Mary Ware Dennett.

The rivalry continued during 1920s and 30s and Sanger, after her initial help in getting *Married Love* published, tried to inhibit Stopes's activities, particularly in the United States, picturing her as a person who had risen through Sanger's help and now tried to impede her work. The antagonism added to Margaret Sanger's organizational troubles and probably made her concentrate even more on her clinical work.

The Birth Control Clinical Research Bureau

Sanger's clinic was vulnerable legally to the accusation of providing a medical service without being licensed to do so. (Such an accusation, however, in defining contraception as a medical service, at least recognized the right of physicians to provide contraceptive advice and service.) The obvious way to strengthen Sanger's legal position was to engage physicians in the work of contraceptive clinics. This was no easy task for several reasons. First, the whole field of medicine dealing with pregnancy and birth occupied an inferior place in the medical profession. For a long time obstetrics had been at best a paramedical field, with the work mainly performed by folk-trained midwives. Over the preceeding two centuries, however, physicians had asserted their dominance and midwives became relegated to an outer fringe. Birth in hospitals became the norm. This change led to a paradoxical result: physicians had achieved dominance and a near monopoly in obstetrics, but the old associations of this activity discouraged them from entering it. Work on pregnancy, birth, and related subjects, what would be called today obstetrics and gynecology, was mainly an adjunct to general practice. Within organized medicine there was a long struggle before obstetrics and gynecology was finally recognized as a medical specialty in 1915 (Arney 1982). Even so, the supply of interested and competent physicians in this field remained limited, and the few who were really qualified were not likely to accept the risky work in a clinic under lay control.

The disinterest of the medical profession in the field of contraception became evident when Margaret Sanger tried to recruit a medical director for her clinic. The most likely specialists, obstetricians and gynecologists, shunned the field and finally Sanger found a public health physician in Georgia, Dorothy Bocker, who had obtained an M.D., but whose main work was in the field of physical education. Even with this deficient background, the position was a quite risky one for Bocker to take: the American Birth Control League could not support the clinic, because, as a membership organization, it was barred by court decision from doing so; harassment by police and voluntary opponents was likely, and it was even possible that Bocker's license to practice would be revoked. She accepted the job, however, an office was found, and Clinton Chance, an English friend of Sanger, provided the initial funds. The Birth Control Clinical Research Bureau started, therefore, as an independent unit under Sanger's control, which eventually was an advantage for her.

The beginning, however, was difficult. Many types of contraceptives were not manufactured in the United States and importation was illegal under the Comstock Act. Margaret Sanger's new husband, J. Noah Slee, was a drug manufacturer with some interests in Canada as well. Through some complicated arrangements between his U.S. and Canadian factories he made it possible for jellies to be made available for the clinics. He was somewhat uneasy, however, about the doubtful legality of his actions. Another of Sanger's admirers, Herbert Simonds, started the Holland Rantos corporation with Slee's financial backing and here contraceptive materials were manufactured. The legality of these acts was not clarified until much later; however, Holland Rantos showed that the manufacture of diaphragms and spermicides could be a profitable enterprise and other manufacturers followed suit. The main motives of the pioneering industrialists was neither the profit motive nor devotion to the cause, but personal attraction to Margaret Sanger.

The supply of at least some contraceptives was thus assured. Yet contraception had the additional practical handicap that data on the different contraceptive techniques were practically nonexistent. The new clinics combined giving needed service and conducting the research required to justify this service. One of the aims of the bureau was to develop and test safe and efficient contraceptives, but for this task Bocker was not well prepared. The records she kept during the first year of the bureau's existence showed that she had used a large number of different contraceptive devices and preparations such that the data on any one of them were not sufficient to draw any definite conclusions. It became clear that she was not up to the task and her relation with the bureau was severed. Fortunately a replacement was soon found.

Dr. Hannah Stone (1893–1941) was a physician married to a gynecologist, Abraham Stone, editor of *Fertility and Infertility*, a leading journal in the field. She had been attached to the Lying-in Hospital in New York, but she gave up this position to work in the Birth Control Clinical Research Bureau. In spite of this, she accepted no pay for her half-time work at the bureau; she saw patients in her private practice and supplemented her advice to clients at the bureau with direct low-cost medical aid.

By all accounts Hannah Stone was the ideal choice for the job. She was an excellent researcher and kept complete records, which proved invaluable to understanding the whole problem of family planning. She also had the personality to inspire confidence in her clients, and as a wife and mother, could elicit data from them that others, such as Dorothy Bocker, had been unable to obtain. In later times her devotion to the cause was shown in her willingness to be a defendant in test cases; further her manuals on contraception, some written together with her husband, became standard educational material in the field.

Under Stone's direction the clinic became a thriving enterprise. Her data showed exactly the characteristics of women who came to the clinic and why they did so. Legally, the clinic could only give contraceptive advice and help for medical reasons, but Stone felt that this restriction made an undue hardship for many women and she marked these records NHR (no health reasons). Fortunately for her, nobody in authority ever checked the records and inquired after the meanings of these initials. Another delicate question was raised by women who were already pregnant. At first the clinic refused any examination once pregnancy was established, but then Sanger decided that these women would be seen at specified times to obtain records on extent and distribution of the problem. With these data she hoped that she could change public opinion and eventually the laws on abortion. No advice on abortion was given, mainly because it was feared that some of the clients were informers sent by the Catholic church.

This fear was not unfounded; the church kept up its campaign against the clinic and everything associated with it. As late as 1929 the clinic was raided by the police, probably under church instigation. A policewoman had gone through the clinic, was judged medically pathological and entitled to treatment, and was given contraceptive advice. The case against the clinic was eventually dismissed, but during the raid police forced their way into rooms where clients were examined; they seized incomplete files and index cards and dumped the contents of other files into trash cans. Some of the women listed on the index cards later received threatening telephone calls and it was feared that the card index was used to identify Catholics who could then be subjected to Church pressure.

The raid had some positive effects for the movement. The clinic enlisted support for its defense from medical organizations as well as the New York Academy of Science, and many groups and individuals were active in its behalf. This strong support showed how far the social climate had swung in favor of family planning or at least in support of the legitimacy of advocating it. Another favorable result was that during the litigation Sanger met an upcoming civil rights lawyer, Morris Ernst (1888–1976), later the leading counsel for the American Civil Liberties Union. He became a lifelong friend of Margaret Sanger and won important cases for the movement. This connection also established a new link with a middle-class liberal coalition whose support Sanger needed, but where she was in competition with influential rivals.

The continuing problems of the clinic remained finances and contraceptive supply. The income from services remained minimal and the clinic was still dependent on grants from friends and from foundations. Sanger obtained some support from Slee, sometimes in exchange for promises that she would spend time with him if she could be relieved of her financial worries. But the best continuing source was the Bureau of Social Hygiene, which was financed by the Rockefeller Foundation. Besides general sympathy with the aims of the clinic the bureau was also trying to do research in the field and by this time Sanger and Stone had the best and most complete records. Cooperation was necessary to obtain the data and support the continuing work of the clinic, which the foundation saw as a data collection activity. During this time research on sexual, reproductive, and contraceptive behavior started to attract attention and this aspect of the clinic's work helped to ensure its prestige.

The provision of contraceptive material persisted as a problem. Although the manufacture of creams and jellies was possible and became quite profitable, distribution still encountered legal obstacles, mainly due to the Comstock Act. Barrier methods, especially condoms, were easier to distribute because they could be marketed as protection against veneral disease. The difficulty was especially noxious because the aim of the clinic was the discovery and testing of new techniques, in order to find contraceptive methods that were safe, reliable, and acceptable, and easy to use for most women. Research on contraceptives, if not their actual use, was seriously hampered.

Courts and Legislation

Women's organizations at the forefront of the movement tried to remedy the legal obstacles to distribution through legislative action, the same path that had achieved victory in the women's suffrage fight. This effort was personified by Mary Ware Dennett; Sanger's impatience with the slowness of the approach was one of the less personal reasons for the break between these two leaders. In the current fight Sanger's distrust of organizational procedures and her sense of urgency were helpful to her, as much as they led to some of her organizational failures in other circumstances.

These two approaches were, of course, not exclusive. Mary Dennett herself had been the center of an early court battle in 1915 about sex education pamphlets. The decision in the case stated that material was not lascivious just because it could lead to sexual arousal, but only if this arousal was its explicit and primary aim. This decision proved to be helpful not only in further arguments about contraception; it became important in the struggle about censorship as well. In 1931 the argument was used in the case *U.S. v. a Book, Ulysses,* which found that James Joyce's novel could not be banned from importation because of its sexually explicit content only, without proof that the author had purely lascivious aims. Here the argument of intent led to the virtual abolition of censorship under the Comstock Act, which in turn helped the efforts of the birth control campaign. This example shows how closely the birth control movement was connected with the civil liberties movement and that a generally favorable climate had arisen allowing joint success. More than a decade elapsed, however, between the Dennett decision in 1915 and the other decisions that grew out of it (Dennett 1926).

The legitimacy of contraception as part of medical practice was gradually recognized through this series of court decisions. Here the assertion for autonomy of the medical profession prevailed; the argument that medical needs should be preeminent and that the physician should be able to prescribe anything necessary for the patient's help proved dominant. The general prestige of professionals and of the medical profession in particular proved to be a match for the desire for the regulation of vice that the Comstock Act had represented. But the decisions up to this point had only legitimized contraceptive education for physicians. But the side of the movement that Sanger represented was more interested in the improvement of contraception and in the acceptance of birth control by society.

The law still provided obstacles here by restraining the manufacture and distribution of contraceptives and especially the introduction of new methods. Margaret Sanger had learned of exciting new developments abroad, but she could not try them out easily in her clinic. She learned of a new kind of pessary, and Hannah Stone offered herself as a test case and had a package mailed to her. It was confiscated by Customs and the resulting litigation, *U.S. v. One Package* (1936) became the landmark case on the field. Morris Ernst, who had since become counsel for the American Civil Liberties Union, prepared an exhaustive brief, citing medical and sociological evidence for birth control, which the Appeals Court judge, Augustus Hand, accepted. The decision affirmed the doctrine that the purpose of the restrictive federal acts had not been to regulate medical relationships; although some material relating to birth control could incite some people sexually—and even if this had been the intent of some purveyors—the material itself clearly had medical and social functions and could only be judged in this way. This decision was not appealed to the Supreme Court and became accepted as the federal guideline on contraception. The mails were now open to the distribution of information about contraceptives and to contraceptives themselves.

This judicial decision and some of those that developed out of it were seen as a great victory for the birth control movement. It was especially important for the dissemination of information to physicians in rural areas who up to then had had to rely on personal contacts with informants in planned parenthood centers. From another point of view, however, with this advance the movement had reached a plateau. It became clear that there were advantages and disadvantages to the strong connection with the medical profession, which Sanger favored but Dennett opposed.

Birth control had become a medical problem and was only subject to the restrictions on the medical profession itself; thus it became exempt from the strictures of federal laws against sexually arousing material. But family planning could not be discussed publicly as an issue of public policy, because public opinion would not allow it. It was felt that birth control should not be hindered in its medical importance, but it could not become part of public debate as an economic and social issue. This limit became apparent when courts supported state laws that limited sale and prescription of contraceptives, leaving the terms of its nonmedical use for the state legislatures to decide. As a nonmedical vehicle contraception could lose the protection as well as the control of the medical profession. The movement thus achieved some legal success, but was still subject to the limits of public opinion.

Public Intervention: Positive and Negative

The twenties was a period during which there was support for the state to interfere negatively, by enjoining acts deemed dangerous to the mores of the society, but in which there was little support for positive public action. These norms, however, gradually changed. The removal of the federal obstacles to the transport of contraceptives accompanied the repeal of the prohibition amendment, the strongest expression of morally restrictive legislation. But the impact of the depression and the coming of the New Deal changed attitudes about social action. This change prepared the way for a general acceptance of positive government action; in the short range some of the New Deal measures resulted in a more favorable position for family planning.

Many public agencies were initiated or expanded during these years. The support or opposition that they gave to the family planning movement depended frequently on the personal views of those in control (Reed 1978). Thus, while an obvious agency to support the movement was the Children's Bureau, especially after the Social Security Act specifically appropriated funds for maternal health and Congress authorized a program to combat venereal disease that could include protection during intercourse, the head of the Children's Bureau, Catherine Lenroot, was adamantly opposed to birth control. She objected in part for the usual religious and moral reasons, but also because she feared a depopulation of the country. She therefore ordered that only a formal negative reply could be given to inquiries about family planning and refused to use any of the funds appropriated for maternal health for family planning.

Margaret Sanger tried to use other channels to introduce family planning into the Roosevelt administration's social program. In particular, she applied to Eleanor Roosevelt, who had been for a long time a quiet supporter of family planning. At the time of America's entry into World War II, when venereal disease had become a problem threatening mobilization, Lenroot finally accepted White House pressure and agreed to transfer the funds on venereal disease control to the Public Health Service. The Surgeon General, Francis Parran, the head of the Public Health Service, was also favorably inclined toward Sanger's work and the funds were freed for their original purpose.

The New Deal reforms were not due to the acceptance of family planning by a liberal administration or a stronger popular pressure exerted in a liberal atmosphere. Again, political and economic liberalism and conservatism do not correlate closely to the progress of the family planning movement. True, Sanger and the other leaders in the movement had better contacts in this administration than previously, but politically the administration was not committed to this issue and, as Lenroot's example showed, also contained opponents in powerful places. In addition, the Democratic party's source of support among Catholics made any open programmatic move in this direction impossible. Family planning did not become either a popular or political issue during this period. But the grounds were prepared on which the movement could succeed: acceptance of an increased role of public social services, even if they were not directly concerned with birth control, and a general liberalization that allowed new alternatives in thought and behavior open to discussion.

Action in Puerto Rico

Although the change was not as fast as some of the supporters of the movement had hoped, the new climate led to some successes, such as that with the Children's Bureau. Another success was the initiation of public family planning programs in Puerto Rico (Back et al. 1960).

Puerto Rico was in a unique position; as a non-self-governing U.S. territory some political considerations carried less weight there than on the mainland. With its Spanish Catholic tradition the church had a strong influence, and attempts at opening birth control clinics in several major cities had failed. But the Great Depression hit Puerto Rico especially hard, as it had been economically depressed and dependent to begin with. The relief agency (PRERA) had had to deal with a range of emergencies, affecting many people; it therefore acquired great power and influence. The administrators could exert this power with considerable leeway: there was little local control and Washington was far away and concerned with closer problems. Thus more experimentation was possible in Puerto Rico than elsewhere (Tugwell 1946).

PRERA started a family planning service in 1935 and within a year, at the height of the program, fifty-three clinics were in operation. The program was not pursued with great energy and the use of the clinics was quite low: there was no outreach or programs to encourage attendance;

as the weekly hours of each clinic were known, a woman's attendance was known to her neighbors, which could be embarrassing (Stycos 1955). Thus the program did not lead to appreciable contraceptive use. But the mere presence of these clinics changed the social climate so that social norms in favor of family planning became accepted. The extent of this change can be seen by the fact that subsequent attempts to reverse this development proved unsuccessful.

A reorganization of federal agencies occurred in 1936, with the successor agency (PRRA) not authorized to continue the program. This was due to pressures in Washington where the administration refused to open the issue of birth control in a presidential election year. On a local level, however, the family planning effort continued. The clinics were taken over by a private organization and the Washington-appointed governor introduced a bill authorizing government support for the teaching and practice of birth control. The tortuous fate of this bill shows the different forces at work in the gradual acceptance of family planning; Puerto Rico can be seen as a miniature laboratory for the family planning movement. The birth control bill was passed by the elected legislature; Governor Blandon Winship was away at the time and it fell to a locally elected official, Menendez Ramos, as acting governor, to decide on its fate. He not only signed it, but issued a strongly worded statement in support of family planning. For this he was excommunicated by the Catholic church, but this action had no effect on public attitudes, which demonstrated the weakness of the church on this issue and, in general, that the official strength of the Catholic church was not translated into public opinion.

Another attempt to oppose the birth control bill was a judicial attack under the Comstock Act. The decision (*U.S. v. de Torres*) upheld the law, mainly on the grounds that the act did not apply to territories. But the judge used the occasion to reaffirm the doctrine of the earlier decision that it was inconceivable that Congress would pass a law interfering with the duty of a physician to safeguard patients' health. Puerto Rico could establish therefore a system of maternal or "prematernal" health clinics that withstood political changes.

The Puerto Rican experience showed that the barriers against further advancement of the movement could be surmounted. The main opponent, the Catholic church, proved itself more symbolic than effective. In a territory whose population was almost exclusively Catholic an elected official could defy excommunication; a party, the Popular Democrats, which supported family planning clinics, came into power and dominated politics in the fifties and sixties. It also showed the importance of strategically placed individuals: the leader of the victorious Popular Democrats, Luis Muñoz Marin, although a nominal Catholic, opposed the church on many political issues; the head of Bureau of Territories and Possessions, Ernest Gruening, was a strong advocate of family planning and decades later was, as a senator, instrumental in making family planning a part of U.S. policies. He was able to insulate the governor from political pressures in Washington. The main effective opposition to family planning had been the influence of church leaders and their political representatives on government officials in Washington; a popular base for this policy had been assumed, which in this case proved to be highly overrated (Gruening 1973).

At the same time, this story showed the limit of an approach directed exclusively on family planning. The legal and political justification for government support was based exclusively on health reasons. In consequence the health department became exclusively responsible for its executions. No one in the department of health had specific responsibility for family planning. The physicians in charge of these programs had, of course, many other responsibilities and thus the effectiveness of the program became dependent on the commitment of the local health officer. It was easy for unsympathetic officials to allow the program to be submerged among other health concerns, just as it was possible for others to mount an effective campaign. In general aid and information for family planning were available for those who wanted them, but they rarely reached those who did need them but had no idea of their existence.

An Individual Health Issue

The Puerto Rican situation was a comparative success for the movement, but it represented the limits the movement had reached. The legal obstacles were abolished one by one, because contraception was recognized as a reputable medical procedure and was protected within the accepted self-determination of the profession; it had lost its pejorative connection with sexual licentiousness. But, outside the doctor-patient relationship, there was no positive value attached to family planning and contraception. Some advances were still possible within this framework, but only if one could mobilize medical support without touching the question of other justifications for family planning.

Support was increased largely through the medical contacts of Margaret Sanger's clinic. Because of her persistent efforts the clinic had a unique set of data on medical and social conditions of pregnancy. Interest in research in the field started to become important and demand for access to these data increased. Financial support became easier to secure because maintaining data of high quality was in the interest of many. Organizations that wanted to contribute to varying aspects of maternal health and birth control became interested in the smooth functioning of the clinic. For instance, the Rockefeller Foundation and its subsidiaries increased their support and gave on a regular basis.

The New Medical Recruits

This new professional stance made possible new linkages with physicians and philanthropists who had come to family planning from their own concerns (Reed 1978). The tradition of physicians who were led through their experience with obstetrics to questioning the current restrictions had started with Knowlton and continued with others. These physicians, from impeccable backgrounds, lent respectability to the movement. Family planning's principal medical ally, starting in the 1920s, was Robert Latou Dickinson (1861–1950).

Dickinson, a physician from a comfortable background, had shown during his training a particular aptitude for anatomical observation and drawing, concentrating especially on the female reproductive system. When he turned to a regular private practice in Brooklyn, he kept up his interests in obstetric problems. Like other concerned physicians before him, he was particularly impressed by the social and medical problems presented by pregnancy and the lack of knowledge to control them. He was acutely conscious of the lack of information among women who needed it most, but he also had to acknowledge a disturbing amount of ignorance among his fellow physicians. This ignorance was aggravated by the low place that obstetric medicine held in the profession. He directed his first public efforts toward remedying this situation.

In the first phase of his career he combined his private practice with vigorous efforts to elevate the position of obstetrics and gynecology within the medical profession. He assumed the presidency of organizations of physicians interested in this field, encouraged publication of teaching and reference material, and promoted specialization and eventual recognition of the field as an important branch of medicine. He succeeded eventually in having obstetrics/gynecology recognized as a medical specialty. This achievement channeled talent, funds, and research into the field, but it also reasserted medical dominance over family planning and contraception.

In the course of these activities Dickinson had encountered Sanger's work, but at this point he rejected any cooperation. Although they had partially the same aims, the backgrounds from which they came were too different to make joint action possible. At first Dickinson was suspicious about the medical supervision of Sanger's clinic. When he learned, however, that Dr. Bocker, the first resident physician at Sanger's clinic, was a graduate of his own medical school, he accepted the clinic's work; at least did not hinder its efforts. At this point, however, despite his increased interest in family planning, he did not engage in any further cooperation.

Dickinson continued his efforts in support of obstetrics, including establishing a base of scientific knowledge on all aspects of female health problems. He himself stayed very active in research and encouraged others to do so. For this purpose he formed the Committee for Maternal Health with a group of other prominent physicians. The committee's primary need was for complete medical records from a large and minimally representative sample of women to establish a baseline for pregnancy and contraceptive experience. Several groups had worked to establish this important data set, among them Sanger's Clinical Research Bureau. Another was the Bureau of Social Hygiene, which, under the leadership of Catherine Davis, published a study of a thousand women. This bureau, like Sanger's clinic, was supported by the Rockefeller Foundation; eventually the Committee on Maternal Health obtained funds from the same source. Thus the research program was in great part maintained by the Rockefeller Foundation (which later supported Kinsey's sex research.) Each participating group had its own strengths and weaknesses. Dickinson's group had high prestige and respectability in the medical profession, but it was also restrained by its rules; these included prohibition of publicity or advertising for subjects or patients, which prevented the committee from finding those in greatest need and restricted it to those patients who sought private physicians with the express desire of obtaining contraceptive information. In contrast, the less medically respectable clinics looked for patients who could profit by the advice and worked therefore with a quite different part of the population. Thanks to Hannah Stone's efforts the Clinical Research Bureau had a large comprehensive file of cases. Eventually Dickinson realized the limits of the conventional medical approach and started to work with Sanger who controlled this valuable resource of case studies.

Thus, by the mid-twenties, Dickinson and Sanger began to cooperate, first in the use of data for research and then for another problem that had been bothering Dickinson—namely the supply of contraceptive devices. One of the aims of the Committee for Maternal Health was to test new and improved contraceptives, but here even medical standing did not help to obtain a sufficient supply of new types of contraceptives. Sanger, however, with her established supply routes, was able to help him here, and Dickinson completed several studies on contraception and brought them to the attention of the medical profession. In this way he succeeded in making work on birth control a recognized part of medical research and practice, even if few physicians were willing to engage in it themselves.

Another individual who advanced the cause of family planning at this time was Clarence J. Gamble (1894–1966) (Williams and Williams 1978). He represented the wealthy philantropists whose ethical principles led them to devote their resources and efforts to social action. Gamble was one of the heirs to a soap manufacturer's fortune, which started with Ivory Soap and developed into the Proctor and Gamble Company. Although in his generation the family had given up the control of the company, each family member was left with considerable capital and income, and also with a sense of duties associated with their privilege. In his college years Clarence Gamble became involved in a wide-ranging network of individuals engaged in social betterment and kept up a voluminous correspondence. He then obtained a medical degree and started an academic career in the Department of Pharmacology at the University of Pennsylvania. His original aim had been basic research. But a concussion received in a plane accident just after he had completed medical school resulted in lack of concentration and persistent exhaustion, accentuating those traits that had been part of his character before the accident. This condition became so pronounced that his supervisor advised him against a research or teaching career. Gamble looked for involvement in other socially valuable activities and was gradually attracted to the question of family planning. Early on, he had an interview with Dickinson, but he was not yet ready to involve himself too much. His interest developed partly out of general considerations, for example, that the danger of the higher fertility of the lower economic classes would overwhelm the dominant stock of the country. He discussed these and related topics with other prominent Philadelphia citizens; they agreed that a program of sex education, family planning, and clinical research would be a valuable contribution to society (Reed 1978).

Gamble did not believe in the welfare state or in dependence on public support; however, he felt committed to use at least one tenth of his considerable wealth for the public good. He wanted to invest most of this money in family planning, but he also wanted to control the way the money was spent. Therefore he did not support only the efforts of Sanger and Dickinson, but he started several clinics on his own, in conjunction with local supporters of planned parenthood. Standing outside the established organizations and impervious to governmental pressures, he did not fit exactly into the medical model to which previous clinical efforts had conformed. In particular, he did not have to draw the line between medical service and education.

Thus Clarence Gamble, the philanthropic capitalist, reintroduced the propagandistic effort that had been the core of the radical movement but was lost when family planning became clinical service. Like the radicals, he had been drawn toward family planning—though from a different direction—not for individual and medical reasons, but because of concerns with large-scale social questions. Gamble's efforts in expanding the movement led him into all kinds of promotional activities, into supporting research for new contraceptives, and into advocacy of new departures. Some of his work was undertaken in cooperation with the Committee for Maternal Health, but later his need for independence reasserted itself and he started his own foundation, the Pathfinder Fund. This fund supported strong advocacy not only of family planning, but also of the development of a national population policy, in accordance with Gamble's own original interests.

The integration of family planning into medical practice had removed many of the legal and social obstacles that had hampered it at the start. The movement had reached a plateau, a climate had been created in which those who knew what they wanted in contraception could obtain it, but in which there was little public outreach. An expansion of the movement to a more powerful position became possible only when certain social factors started to work in its favor.

Part 3

Transformation

Chapter Six

Becoming a Norm

The alliance with the medical profession was profitable for the family planning movement. It brought protection from state interference, wide permission for dissemination of information, provision of services, and even manufacture and importation of contraceptives. But this advance was bought at a price. Medical standards required serious limitations. Medicine is a profession, not a business; physicians could offer professional advice to patients, but not market a product or an idea. Only a limited, specially trained group of people can take responsibility for medical service, but such training is unnecessary in the case of contraception because the actual procedures are quite simple and no arcane skill is required.

The movement had dismantled many of the obstacles in the way of family planning; contraception was accepted as a legally and technically possible method and it was unlikely that its still powerful opposition could smother it completely. But the movement had lost the drive that had led the pioneers to fight such opposition. The medical connection meant that contraception was available for the individuals who wanted it, but practitioners were not driven by social concern. By the 1930s most people, even those who opposed them in principle, accepted the existence of birth control clinics and the fact that some people used them. They were rarely looked at as social disgrace, but nor were they viewed as a path to achieve important social aims. Medical practice deals with individual needs, not the needs of society. If the movement had further aims, or wanted to return to the aims that had given it its fervor in the early days, it needed a commitment to innovative social values.

Population Decline and Eugenics

Here we have to take up again the story of the demographers. The influence of the demographers at the start of the family planning movement in the United States was hindered by their avoidance of the question of how excess fertility and population increase could be prevented. In England the Malthusian League tried to combine demographic interests with advocacy of contraception but, as we have seen, the league's politically right-wing stance interfered with links to some of the radical advocates of family planning.

Thus, while demographic considerations provided motivating forces for the movement, they were separated from the planning activities on the personal level. The mechanics of immediate individual action and concern with remote dangers to the society could not be coordinated; the practical family planning approach could work negatively, removing legal obstacles, but it could not give the positive impetus required to make it a social goal.

The political economists and demographers would not and could not push the movement in this direction, principally because the danger of overpopulation had receded. This was the situation during the nineteenth and early twentieth centuries. Population expansion had not led to lack of subsistence, because improvement of agriculture and worldwide expansion of land under cultivation more than made up for population increase in the short run. Especially in the industrialized countries it was clear that food was available and that hunger was a question of the distribution of wealth. But even in the rest of the world technical successes did not seem to make overpopulation an imminent danger.

The population problem became not a question of numbers of people in general, but of the kind or quality of people. This concern was expressed in the relations between nations in the early twentieth century, seen in the cry of "yellow danger," which signified whites' fear of being overrun by the masses of China and Japan, or in the French fear of depopulation in comparison with its presumptive foe, Germany (Spengler 1938, Nye 1984). These fears led to an attempt at population increase in the countries that felt themselves threatened, that is to pronatalistic policies. More difficult and powerful for a time was the discussion within a country, that the wrong kinds of people increased too much and the right kind too little. The "right" and "wrong" could be defined ethnically, as in the fear in the United States that the population of northwest European origin would be overwhelmed by that from southern or eastern Europe, or by differences in ability. This popular argument has reappeared in many guises; it is an outgrowth of both social conditions and biological theories. Such ideas, which formed the ideological base of eugenic social movements, have had an intricate relationship with family planning and must therefore be discussed here in greater detail (Kevles 1985).

Malthus's hypothesis that population will always strain the limits of its subsistence had one important influence: Charles Darwin (1962, 1969) credits his reading of the passages in *Principles of Population* at a crucial time for his discovery of the law of survival of the fittest, one of the pillars of evolutionary theory. The biological law had its ancestry in social reasoning and this connection in the application of Darwinian theory to human affairs has persisted. Darwinism, even while its scientific principles were controversial or misunderstood, was soon applied to social problems. Concepts like evolution, selection of the fittest, or survival value could be easily applied to human differences. The rise of neo-Malthusianism at the end of the nineteenth century became quickly involved with the eugenics movement, which tried to apply the principles of evolution to human betterment.

The originator of the eugenics movement and of the term *eugenics* itself was Francis Galton, a cousin of Darwin. He was financially independent and devoted his time to his many scientific interests, which included psychology, statistics, and geographic exploration. One of his particular interests was the preservation of superior traits, which he referred to as genius. He investigated the family connections of talented people and published his first major work, *Hereditary Genius,* in 1869. His continuing work on the inheritance of mental characteristics led him then to initiate the field of eugenics, devoted to the improvement of the human race.

The relation between eugenics and family planning can be understood by distinguishing positive and negative eugenics. The former will encourage people with superior characteristics to have more offspring; the latter tries to decrease the offspring of people with undesirable traits. Malthus's own ideas partly fit in with eugenic concerns, but partly opposed them. His fundamental principle, that improvement in welfare of the poor would lead to their increased fertility until the original level of poverty was reached again, fed the concern of eugenicists, especially since many of them assumed the poor to have undesirable traits. Nevertheless, Malthus's remedies and even those of the neo-Malthusians, who accepted contraception, had little appeal for eugenicists. Since delayed marriage and restraint are methods mainly applicable to the middle and upper classes, dissemination of information about contraception could easily have undesirable consequences from a eugenic point of view.

Thus the relation between eugenics and family planning became quite involved. If one knows which parts of the population are desirable and which are not, two paths are open to improve the genetic stock. One can increase the reproductive effectiveness of the desirable segment or decrease that of the undesirable. The latter can be objectionable from moral and political points of view and has been stated bluntly as an objective only in extreme conditions (i.e., obvious genetic defects) or by extreme, for instance racist, groups; it can lead to genocide. Some family planners offered a kind of compromise: by providing clinics and advice for the poor they could claim they were spreading contraception and decreased fertility to all sectors of the population and thus trying to eliminate the dysgenic effects of family planning. Some leaders of the family planning movement, especially Marie Stopes in England, were quite convinced eugenicists as well; others were willing to accept allies where they could—often family planning literature contained eugenic arguments.

An important thrust of the eugenic movement was to encourage the increase of favorable strains, which meant improvement of the fertility of the upper classes or of exceptionally healthy families. In the United States the movement received an impetus from the results of the testing of recruits in World War I, which showed significant differences in intelligence (as measured by the Army Alpha Intelligence Test) in ethnic groups. These results furthered the passage of the Immigration Act of 1923, which set lower quotas for immigration from central and southern Europe than from western and northern Europe, as indicated by the test results. In this way data on ability was used to further ethnically motivated policies; they also led to such other policies as compulsory sterilization laws, which were attempts at negative eugenics. The strengthened eugenics movement in the 1920s was, however, especially visible in its attempts at positive eugenics, in encouraging high fertility among those groups they deemed desirable. This effort led to a variety of techniques, including publicity for eugenic achievements, contests for large healthy families, and warnings that nations overrun by genetically weaker groups would decline. Positive eugenics did lead to a fear that population might decline; here demographers and political economists who favored higher fertility of some population groups were not allies of the family planning movement, which wanted to control fertility.

Fertility did in fact decline in the United States, partially to changing female roles in the 1920s, the "jazz age," and later to the depression, reaching a low point in the late 1930s. This trend, in conjunction with reduced immigration, tended to stabilize population size, but it also heightened the differences among ethnic and racial groups. There were strong differences in fertility between whites and nonwhites and between protestants of northern European heritage and other white groups, between families of high and low education, and also among corresponding occupational groups. Thus the concern of scholars and policy makers in this field (who themselves came principally from the sectors favored by eugenicists), was not with the overall increase of the population, but with the differences in fertility that might lead to a threat to desirable population distribution. A similar argument was made about the overall population size of the country in comparison with other countries, that a smaller population might lessen the nation's power in the world; again the threat of nations with different racial stock (such as the "yellow danger") was emphasized.

Thus, in spite of the willingness of family planning advocates to adapt to eugenic reasoning, there remained a divergence between those sponsoring efforts on the individual level and those concerned with demography. Family planning workers stressed the importance of contraception for the individual woman and for the welfare of the child and family. As far as social demographic efforts were concerned, there was no similar consensus.

Research on Demography

Detailed demographic studies, supplementing the clinical studies of contraceptive use, were also motivated by a fear of population decline, specifically the decline of the favored ethnic group. The principal object of these first micro-demographic studies was the analysis of the problem of low fertility. The first major detailed study begun in the mid-thirties concentrated on the population decline of the white protestant population of a small city in the American heartland, Indianapolis. The study used a newly developed methodology, which has become familiar as the sample survey. It was based on a random sample of the population and the data were collected with closed-end, forced choice questions. The researchers assumed that questions on contraceptives were too private, but aspirations on number of children and the sources of these aspirations could be investigated in detail. Because of delays in introducing the new technique and the outbreak of the war the study was only completed much later, under different circumstances. One of the indirect results of this undertaking was the assembly of a group of demographers with interest in fertility together with a group of sociologists who were becoming skilled in survey research techniques. Because of the long time that this study took to complete new recruits with different scientific backgrounds joined the research team and the study was analyzed in many ways not thought of by the original research team. This course of events established a tradition of cooperation among demographers, sociologists, and social psychologists, which has given fertility control its particular relation to social research (Whelpton and Kiser 1946–58).

World War II changed many accepted ideas on population control, as it did so many other social conditions. The devastation of the war itself brought about actual food shortages in many areas of the world and made the idea that population could outrun food supplies more realistic. For a while even the European nations encouraged emigration, fearing they would be unable to support their own population. But even more influential was the impact of the combination of hunger, poverty, and high population density in East and South Asia, the Carribbean, and other parts of the world.

American attention was directed to many of these areas as a consequence of broadened knowledge acquired during the war and the generally rising belief in the interconnection of all humanity, summarized in the popular slogan of "one world." The leadership in the reconstruction efforts fell to the United States where various government agencies became involved. At the same time the eugenic movement had fallen into disrepute, due in great part to its connection with Nazi racist ideas. Thus, although much of the attack on overpopulation was made in the non-Western areas, great care was taken that this effort could not be ascribed to eugenic or other invidious distinctions among different population groups.

Of course, some people had been worried during this time about excessive population increase. It was evident that an almost exponential expansion in population size could not continue indefinitely and that at least in this sense Malthus was undeniably correct. The European experience had shown, however, that decrease of fertility could stabilize population size after the rapid increase that resulted from improvements in medical knowledge, sanitation, and nutrition.

The demographer Warren Thompson developed in these years the theory of demographic transition, which sought to generalize this experience of population stabilization in industrialized countries into a general law. In an influential article published in 1929 he defined three stages through which a society's population passes: the original one where high fertility is compensated by high mortality; a transition phase in which mortality declines through improvement in living conditions, leading to rapid population increase; and the third stage in which the population is stabilized through reduction in fertility. Industrialized countries had reached the third stage and it was assumed that other countries that were entering or had entered the transition phase would eventually do so. Although this reduction in fertility depended on use of some form of contraception, the theory assumed that the introduction of birth control would accompany social changes and no particular intervention was necessary.

The pressures of the time raised additional questions. The large population increase in many countries, especially in East Asia, made it doubtful that the pace of the European transition would be sufficient to avoid large dislocations. In addition there were doubts whether the experience could be repeated in the way the theory had proposed. In the Western industrialized countries the reduction of mortality had depended on the gradual introduction through trial and error of many cumulative improvements in living standards. This period had extended over two centuries and the accompanying decrease in fertility led to gradual stabilization without too severe dislocation. In the newly developing countries the wholesale importation of advances in sanitation, medicine, and nutrition led to an abrupt increase in population while decrease in fertility would likely be much slower if it only depended on the indirect effects of social changes. Such gradual demographic transitions would be too slow to prevent severe dislocation. Considerations of this kind led demographers to interest themselves in interventionist programs; they did so with extreme caution at first.

The Rockefeller Mission

An early involvement of demographers in population control problems was a mission sent by the Rockefeller Foundation to several Asian countries under the leadership of Marshall Balfour, the director of Far Eastern activities for the foundation. Frank Notestein was the main demographic consultant. In an initial report he revised and extended the demographic transition theory to take account of these new conditions. It seemed that the decline of the birth rate after the decline of the death rate was not an isolated phenomenon in the West, but was widespread. The same social and economic factors that decreased mortality brought about a leveling of population increase. For example, improvement in the condition of women may reduce their mortality through better information, education, abolition of child marriages, and generally better treatment; but these same changes would reduce fertility through late marriage and availability of career alternatives to childbearing. Notestein admitted that imposition from the outside of only some of the factors that had been present in the West might produce disruption; if social conditions for family planning are absent, introduction of contraceptives, especially from a foreign sponsor, could be counterproductive. East Asians were aware of Western concern about the "yellow danger." On the other hand, without contraceptives one could not expect population increase to level off in the reasonable future. The Rockefeller mission concluded, however, that it was preferable to work on general modernization and let actual family planning develop in due time (Memorandum, Rockefeller Archive, Pocantico Hills, N.Y.).

The experience of the investigation reconfirmed this cautious point of view. On the one hand there was a need to control population size before population expanded beyond food production, but on the other hand one had to be very careful in limiting oneself to a locally supported, integrated program. Thus this approach of demographers to neo-Malthusianism (Malthus's theory plus contraception) tried to avoid the aggressive initiatives that the family planning movement had undertaken. The recommendation of the group were correspondingly cautious; the three prongs of the proposed program included raising the marriage age, improving the standard of living, and elimination of institutional limitations on contraception. The prime emphasis was directed toward increasing the underlying motivation for family limitation; in the absence of restraints against family planning it was assumed that fertility decrease would come about naturally.

In addition, the report stressed the need for better data collection; this recommendation could be readily implemented: financial aid to census agencies and consultation by competent demographers were soon arranged. Direct advocacy of contraception, however, either through influence on motivation or provision of services, was avoided. Even during the trip itself the delicate nature of the issue became evident; local complaints about interference were matched by speeches by American Catholic officials.

Balfour was the senior author of the report (Balfour et al. 1950), which was widely distributed under the auspices of the Rockefeller Foundation. Compared with the activities of family planners the report was cautious;

but its reception showed how far family planning was still only tolerated and not fully accepted. The report was criticized for not emphasizing more the neutral topics, that is, principally development and welfare issues. Approaching contraception, even indirectly, and proposing population control as an ultimate goal was considered at best bad manners and at worst unwarranted imperialism; some might even have called it genocide if the term had been in general use at the time.

In spite of all the reservations in the report and in spite of its reception, which disappointed many of the commission members, the mission was a crucial step in the history of the family planning movement. Because the trip did not include any representatives of the family planning movement at the time, the members of the group had to discover the importance of systematic introduction of contraception on their own. Most of them were demographers and accustomed to looking at the national situation in each country, estimating the general direction of social and economic development that was indicated. Their training led them to act as if they were completely unaware of the personal problems that lead people to control their own fertility. If professional family planners had been present to raise these issues, arguments in favor of contraception might have looked like special pleading; but here demographers were able to convince themselves of the importance of the birth control movement for economic concerns.

In effect, the report misestimated two trends in its predictions. It underestimated the population increase that occurred in the next decades, although even the numbers that they projected seemed to the report's authors to lead to disaster. On the other hand, it overestimated the resistance to introduction of contraception: Japan, as well as Taiwan, South Korea, and Singapore have become the leading advocates of a strong, active population control policy. This outcome did not detract from the influence that the demographers wielded in the subsequent story of family planning. Even with considerable public support of family planning, population increased to unimagined heights; but this increase did not have as disastrous consequences in East Asia as had been feared. Keeping these events in mind we can assess the impact of the conjunction between economic consideration and concern with family planning.

The Rockefeller suggestions that were followed up immediately were the improvement in data collection and the documentation of the population problem. This may look like a small beginning, but one must remember the great effort that the pioneers in the clinics had had to exert to obtain any reliable data on their clients and the need for the services of the clinics. The data collected by the demographers were not specifically directed toward contraception but rather included information about size and distribution of the population, age and sex ratios, and economic and social needs. These data later became the bases for arguments for population control. But what might have been even more important, working with these figures sensitized the demographers, economists, and sociologists to look at population size, birth rates, and family conditions as issues that could not be ignored, but that were amenable to planned change.

The obvious distress of the Far Eastern countries and their population density made them the principal target for agitation for population control. The immediate postwar atmosphere may have played a role here. Population pressure had been blamed or seen as a justification for Japanese expansionism, leading to the Pacific war. Similarly, dealing with this pressure could be seen either as continuing the war or as ameliorating the root causes. To do this the organizations that had been working on human betterment and worldwide planning had to enter a new field.

The Population Council

In spite of the original sponsorship of the exploration by the Rockefeller Foundation—or perhaps because of the controversial reception of the report—the foundation's officials were reluctant to enter the field of population planning. The foundation had had a cooperative relationship with the family planning movement, giving continuing support to Margaret Sanger's clinics. The interest had been directed, however, more toward sexual health problems and sexual morality; the Rockefeller-sponsored institution in this field was called the Bureau of Social Hygiene. The combination of this history of involvement with the traditional work on social and economic development was not sufficient to set in motion a concerted effort on population planning.

John D. Rockefeller III was, however, personally committed to this issue; he therefore used his own funds to found a new organization, the Population Council (Population Council 1978). The council was able to initiate and support pioneering programs in population control. Its statement of aims and activity concentrated specifically on problems arising from population size and distribution. Although most of them were couched in terms of furthering training and data collection, and encouraging local centers of professional activities, it did mention "social, ethical and moral implications of contraceptive methods" and included "studies of the factors governing family size and the modes of their change" among its activities.

But what may have been in the long run a more important effect, it showed by its existence and sponsorship that questions of population control and family planning could become part of the general agenda and so served as a model for the involvement of other organizations and opinion leaders. It was the first foundation that concentrated exclusively on the population question. Previously two small foundations, the Scripps Foundation and the Millbank Memorial Fund, had included population concerns among their activities (mainly directed toward public health) and helped in establishing two population research centers, at Miami University (Ohio) and at Princeton University. The council, by contrast, concentrated its considerable resources on population questions in all their ramifications. It was organized into two divisions, biomedical and demographic. This combination acknowledged again that there was an individual, contraceptive dimension to the population question. It also made it easier for the Population Division, which was influenced by traditional demographers, to engage in new ventures of family planning. In addition, both divisions had theoretical and applied concerns: the bio-medical division sponsored studies of the reproductive system as well as the development of new contraceptives, and the demographic division worked on the collection and improvement of population data as well as the promotion of family planning. This made it possible for intellectual and financial supporters to restrict themselves to noncontroversial subjects, perhaps until they were convinced that applied practice was equally acceptable and important.

True to its origin, the Population Council turned its attention initially to foreign, worldwide problems, a position it has maintained largely to the present day. The most striking problem had been in East Asia, but the scale there was too vast to be tackled directly. Hence the council turned its attention to the overpopulated Caribbean Islands. Here there were natural laboratories, limited by the size of the islands. In addition, islands make the threat of overpopulation particularly graphic; in fact, many of the most successful programs in population control have been instituted on islands (Puerto Rico, Taiwan, Singapore, Mauritius, even Japan), especially in the early years, and have found comparatively little political resistance. But the Caribbean had additional importance for the American scene: besides being closer and more noticeable for this reason alone, immigration from these places started to become a social problem, which made many Americans aware of the population pressure there.

Family Planning and Population Control

In the foreign studies the separate interests of population control and family planning, that is, work on the social or on the individual aspect of the problem, became more and more apparent. The initial position of the demographers was very careful, as we have seen. Their work complemented the previous efforts of the family planning movement. Family planners, from Place to Sanger, had attacked existing restraints at great personal risk. In contrast, the demographers' new approach tried to use established or assumed paths of social change to prepare the ground for the acceptability of family planning.

While the family planners started with generally radical ideas and gradually moved to a respectable reformist activity, the population control advocates started from an abstract theoretical position on reconstruction and gradually accepted the need for action by individuals toward individuals. The contrast between the two positions persisted and was never completely resolved.

Some of these contrasts can be seen in the documents of a series of conferences that Rockefeller and his associates arranged during the years 1952–53 (documents deposited in the Rockefeller Archive, Pocantico Hills, N.Y.). Out of these meetings arose eventually the organization of the Population Council. The joint conferences continued, designed to make plans for common action, but the preparation, the agenda, and subsequent correspondence showed deep disagreements on tactics and probably on basic values. One symptom of this conflict was an agreement to keep the meetings that did occur confidential, and to postpone decisions on publications, proceedings, and dissemination of results. Correspondence between Frederick Osborn, the executive vice-president of the Population Council, and Paul Henshaw, the director of research of the Planned Parenthood Federation, shows some of the elements of this conflict. It was an achievement to reach an agreement that "control of fertility by physiologic means. . . is a tangible research approach," but the advisability of promoting these approaches remained controversial. Here the main arena of discussion was the question of how far public meetings and writing should restrict themselves to factual information and how far views based only on opinions should be allowed. The borderline between facts and opinions is, of course, an unresolved issue in philosophy and sociology of science; but the discussion really implied a new approach to family planning.

The whole development of the Planned Parenthood League had been based on the conviction that personal choice in birth control practices had an unquestioned positive value and that the main social problem was provision of information and services and removal of obstacles to doing so. The general question of overpopulation was of little real concern; if the family planners thought about it all, they assumed that, given adequate information and means, individuals in the aggregate would act as rationally as experience had shown that individual families did. It was not a question of changing people, but of giving them the means to reach their own goals. The population people who saw a global peril were more concerned about large-scale effects. They also saw that different avenues could achieve population limitation. Some of these courses of action were unorthodox and potentially dangerous, such as extreme government actions or intensive propaganda campaigns. With a new definition of the problem, demographers were proposing a kind of social engineering and were wary of arousing opposition. Also they wanted to be clear about their own future steps. By making population stabilization a public concern they were inviting unprecedented change and they knew it. But such theorists seemed somewhat cautious to the family planners who had worked hard and courageously on a more limited agenda.

The establishment of the Population Council was of course not the only event that changed the position of the family planning and population control movement. But it was a major part of this change. The main development in the decade or so following World War II was the inauguration of a new phase of the movement where people were coming to realize that population was a problem that had to be dealt with. From this period on public debates on overpopulation were possible, with powerful advocates on either side of the issue and contraception seen as an important part of the solution. In fact, the burden of proof was now on the opponents of contraception to show alternative means of reaching the goal. This shift brought new actors, new conditions, and new strategies to the fore.

The Positive Climate

Success for a social movement needs two different conditions, each requiring different approaches and protagonists. In the beginning a movement is faced with social opposition to personal acts. To be accepted by society, however, the movement has to make the individual actions acceptable; this may require heroic and self-sacrificial measures. But the movement will only succeed if its actions do not depend on unusual individuals. In order for these acts to be accepted as normal behavior, they must acquire some basis in the belief system of the society. It is not necessary that the activities be rooted in universally recognized norms, but they should be placed in a general theoretical framework that is socially acceptable. In the history of the family planning movement this moment arrived when population size was seen as a matter of social concern.

In the family planning movement these two phases were carried by two separate groups, those concerned with family planning and those concerned with population control. The struggle against restrictions on individual actions was carried by heroes and heroines who consciously violated rules and laws to provide information on birth control, distributed contraceptives, and established clinics. They acquired fame and notoriety and their names, from Francis Place and Amy Besant to Margaret Sanger and Marie Stopes, form the roll call of the pioneers. On the other hand, their activities were tied to different sets of ideas, many of which, like anarchism, remained extremely marginal in the society. They also abandoned some of these beliefs, trying to bring family planning into a more favorable light. Thus, one by one, they overcame the most visible obstacles to work on family planning.

Family planners had to enter opportunistic alliances with many groups whose help could be useful or whose opposition could smother their activities. These alliances culminated in work with the medical profession, which was naturally concerned, but tended to subordinate family planning to its central interests of curing diseases. Family planning work was still risky, but it was mainly concerned with helping individual distress and little linked to the major social concerns of the time.

The social acceptance of family planning was achieved by those concerned with population control. Their concerns were not connected with any specific actions and were mainly expressed in theoretical discussions, which could also become heated, but only in an academic sense. Their activity did not lead to spectacular events, such as police raids and show trials, and the protagonists of these ideas were less likely to catch the public eye. (Malthus was an exception, but his name was associated, unwarrantedly, with contraception). The continued discussion, first in professional journals, then in serious periodicals, and finally in the mass media, made concern with overpopulation a valid issue, opposed to admiration for population expansion. True, some of the argument was directed toward control of the population increase of outsiders, but gradually the view became acceptable that overpopulation as such was a problem. This view has become accepted even in official publications. It may not be the dominant one; communities still complain, if census data show that they have lost population. But at least it has provided a consistent framework that has given family planning a role in national concerns.

Work in producing change in social norms is not spectacular, but in retrospect the effects of this change look abrupt and striking. The discussion in publications about ultimate ends did not bring individuals to public prominence and the responsible scholars who initiated and continued this discussion are not generally known, but individuals such as Frank Notestein, Marshall Balfour, Clyde Kiser, Kingsley Davis, Joseph Spengler, Frederick Osborn, and Oskar Harkavy have had respectable, sometimes eminent, careers. Their work and influence on social norms is not associated with their names and each individual link of their work with change in norms would be hard to trace. Their cumulative influence looks, in retrospect, like a spontaneous social trend, but it shows how changing norms can eclipse individual actions.

Chapter Seven

New Directions

A new position for the family planning movement can be dated to the period following World War II. Family planning was no longer the peculiar concern of a few dedicated souls, fighting against the dominant forces in society. It became seen as a possible part of a program to solve major recognized problems in society. Comprehensive data on family planning were not available until the 1960s. In national studies in 1965, two-thirds of married couples were using contraception, and more than 80 percent had ever used them at some time (Ryder and Westoff 1971).

The threat of overpopulation took hold of the popular imagination with surprising rapidity. The term *population explosion* gained common currency; research and action to deal with this impending disaster did not need special justification. The immediate goal of the family planning movement—available contraception for all individuals—stood to gain by this change in outlook. But the movement itself was transformed. Its aim was no longer solely to give people the possibility of family planning; more and more the objective became to extend the use of family planning for the common good of society. An important new departure was to learn how this could be done. Redirection of aims needed new kinds of knowledge.

New Kinds of Knowledge

An early sign of the new phase of the movement was in the redirection of research. One may think that facts are neutral, that their accumulation will help to illuminate problems and give more choices for their solution. As we have seen, however, introduction of new knowledge may be an early step toward social change; the first conflicts over contraception were fought over the question of assembling and disseminating facts about human reproduction. When population control became a national concern, then the contributions of the behavioral and social sciences were needed for an understanding of education, influence, and social change. With more funds available for research on family planning and population control, the choice of topics for study and major support for it became more than a neutral theoretical question.

Although scientific progress in all fields connected with family planning could now progress, limits still existed. Some of these limits were financial: many organizations were still reluctant to support a field that in informal conversation was still referred to as "pornographic research." Especially the federal government would not support research that was clearly identified with contraception. These restraints influenced the kind of topics that would be supported, curtailing those that transcended established limits. Even the supposedly quite objective course of science was directed and limited by social norms.

The debate about what could be studied was more pronounced in social than in biomedical research. The latter had the neutral-seeming goal of better understanding the reproductive system; only later—starting in the 1970s, when it led to genetic engineering and artificial reproduction—did it reach the limits of the permissible. Social research, however, was more quickly engaged in value questions when deciding what could be studied: the policy decision of what should be done to promote family planning was always in the background. Was the purpose of the movement to give people the means to control their own fertility or was it to influence their goals as well? How this question was answered determined how far research could be directed toward policies to induce people to limit the size of their families. The official point of view pronounced by family planners was that they promoted freedom of choice, especially as long as this freedom was limited by laws and police action. But the choice made by people with superior power and status can have far-reaching implications by example or more or less subtle means of influence and coercion. Even the endorsement of views by individuals and groups who can serve as models becomes a powerful means of promoting conformity (Kelman 1958). Here research may soon be controversial.

Accumulation of Information

Early research of the postwar period concentrated on ascertaining the demographic facts of possible target populations. Some of this work had been undertaken previously, but all researchers in the field had to overcome a reluctance to write openly about questions of sex and to take scientific study of all aspects of sexual behavior as a serious professional endeavor. Thus it was an achievement that the Committee for Maternal Health charged a sociologist, Norman Himes, with assembling data on contraceptive practices through the ages; his *History of Medical Contraception,* published in 1936, documented the long history of contraceptives in medical practice and showed that important facts and ideas could be gleaned from neglected sources. Work on current contraceptive practice had been done in specialized studies of medical and clinical experience. Here again the main obstacle to getting more data was the general belief that these topics were too personal to be discussed in short interviews with a representative population; we have seen that the early demographic study of fertility, the Indianapolis Study, avoided questions on contraceptive practice and restricted itself to desired and achieved family size. The breakthrough in this regard came from a zoologist, Alfred Kinsey, who with two associates, collected data on sexual behavior from a large sample of the American public.

Kinsey's extreme precautions in assuring confidentiality and his ingenious methods to obtain reasonably representative samples show the uneasiness that even scientists felt in approaching these topics. The three researchers took down their notes in a private code that only they could interpret; a great part of their sample consisted of the membership of clubs that had used some peer pressures to encourage members to participate in the study; population groups that could not be sampled in this way were recruited in other ways, for example, from hitchhikers. Many of these expedients in recruiting subjects cast doubts on the validity of the results. But Kinsey took the first step in showing that information on sexual and contraceptive behavior could be obtained through regular social research procedures.

Kinsey's example led to the initiation of a number of studies on the general population and removed the clinical bias of the studies that had been done up this point. Therefore, we now have data on national use of family planning since this time. As is often the case, the collection of information was valuable in itself and made further progress in this field easier. Once the results of Kinsey's studies and of his successors became public knowledge, the conduct of future studies became easier; even more significant was the gradual removal of barriers from these topics in ordinary discourse. Frequently in the history of the family planning movement the fight against suppression of the material related to birth control was associated with general attacks on censorship, especially of sexually explicit material. Here a similar informal mechanism was at work: research in this field and its dissemination accompanied more general openness about sexual topics in literature, mass media, and general conversation, and this in turn helped the activities of the different branches of the family planning movement. Expansion of knowledge had its own dynamic effect.

The same questions about the possibility of conducting research with the general population on sex and contraception recurred each time information was collected in a new setting. Again and again the same sequence occurred: first it was argued that the subject was unapproachable because it was outside the pale of discourse and knowledge. Once this barrier was overcome, it became apparent that the obstacle existed socially, but not on an individual level. That is, there were taboos within society against discussing sex, but many men and women were actually quite ready to talk about their opinions, practices, and desires. This experience was repeated in Puerto Rico, the Caribbean Islands, Latin America, East and South Asia, the Middle East and Africa, as well as in the industrialized nations. In many cases discussion of sexual behavior and contraception with interviewers was the first step in making people receptive to family planning. In the experiments in introducing family planning, discussed below, this effect of mere discussion was so pronounced among some respondents that it complicated the design: a traditional experimental control condition, including pre- and post-interviews and no educational program, was so effective in introducing contraception with some participants that additional control groups without pre-interviews had to be included (Hill, Stycos, and Back 1959, Stycos and Back 1965). Eventually, gathering of data from any society, independent of assumed cultural, religious, or social conditions became so routine that they were simply called KAP (knowledge, attitude, practice) studies.

The repeated process of branching into new areas helped in securing support of behavioral research. The research agencies, within a few years, accepted the fact that important data could be collected in the course of standard social research; this helped in understanding the dimensions of the need for family planning, but it also freed scientists from dependence on clinic populations. This extension of research could involve all kinds of new application of behavioral science; research was no longer confined to the methodology of data collection in interviews, but relied also on theories and methods of influence, group pressure, mass media effects, learning, and attitude change.

These new developments brought a new question into focus: not what could be studied, but what should be studied; questions of values and goals started to determine the course of research. Again, the progress of research, especially in the social sciences, mirrored the advance of the movement in society.

It is significant that the early concern of research was directed toward contraception; this reflected the thrust of the family planning movement, which had always asserted the importance of the means, while leaving decisions of fertility to the families concerned. In fact, this attitude corresponded to the reliance on the civil liberties argument of promoting freedom of information and freedom of choice. These claims had been very valuable in the work with physicians who would advise a woman to use contraception for her health, but would not advocate a general program of family limitation for the good of society. The great change in social support and opening of new sources of support had come, however, just from this argument. Family planning became popular because it limited population size. It became clear that the desires of individual families might have to be subordinated to social aims.

Dilemmas of Social Research

The start of the social research model followed the planned parenthood idea. It was important to learn whether people wanted to control their family size, whether they knew how to go about it, and how they could be helped to do so. The appropriate use of this research would then be to disseminate the information that people needed to reach their aims and then to give them help in using this information. This approach fit the rhetoric of free choice, which had been effective in dismantling many of the overwhelming obstacles to the work of the pioneers in family planning. It was not just empty rhetoric, however; many adherents believed free choice to be the essence of family planning, and in fact planned parenthood clinics gave advice in overcoming sterility.

The population control approach is at first glance not too different from the family planning model; if the individual aims added up to optimal population change, than purely informational campaigns would lead to socially desirable results. But this neat congruence of reasonable people with social aims was not guaranteed. It became clear that it might be necessary, from a population control point of view, to induce people to change their desires to have children. This question has been debated in the scientific community, among social agencies and policy makers.

Questions about population, which had previously interested only a small group of demographers, had become important social problems and more data in the field were needed. This renewed effort coincided with the abrupt increase in social science research in the postwar years, and the application of its new techniques gave additional insights to those obtained from traditional demographic methods. Survey methods were improved and adapted to delicate topics; they were also extended to use in other cultures where further difficulties were anticipated. Many experts began to wonder how far questionnaires could be extended. Could a mandate to do research on family planning include collection of data on sexual habits and personal histories and exact descriptions of contraceptive methods? While this question was still being discussed, the introduction of new methods of social engineering suggested even bolder steps.

An Example of the Social Research Model

Different public and private agencies entered the field of population control and family planning. Frequently interest was motivated by a specific country or locality. In addition to their importance for the country itself, the studies were also designed as demonstration projects. Places of limited size could serve as models for work in other countries, especially the large countries of South and East Asia.

An early application of the model was a sequence of studies in the Carribean, namely in Puerto Rico and Jamaica, the main research effort lasting from 1951 to 1959. The two places had limited size, similar climate, and agricultural resources in common, but they differed in important respects. In Puerto Rico the political situation was favorable for population work. The island had obtained limited self-government (from the United States) in 1948; the elected government was favorable toward family planning, but had proceeded carefully because of the strength of the Catholic church and the traditional view of the Hispanic family which was opposed to family planning. But, because of the political association with the United States, practical and logistical problems of research were easier than in other places and therefore family planning could be studied here in a new context.

Jamaica, by contrast had been a British colony for three hundred years, but was on its way to independence. The population was mainly Black, descendants of slaves, and showed strong English influence; in particular the Church of England was the dominant religion, with a minority of Catholics. Two parties vied for political control and alternatingly tried to avoid family planning as a political issue or used it to hurt their opponents. The family organization was quite labile; English Victorian ideals had been imposed on the offspring of plantation society who had different values (Blake 1961).

Preliminary studies, undertaken in Puerto Rico, had little direct connection with birth control. A general sociological study by Paul Hatt and his associates (1952) was designed to study the social structure of the country as far as it was relevant to family planning. A short time later a set of family studies was initiated at the University of Puerto Rico under the general direction of Reuben Hill. The first study in this series, by David Landy, was an anthropological field study of child rearing that provided background information, such as different treatment of boys and girls, that could be important to family planning (Landy 1960).

In the next step the university, through its research center, sponsored an intensive study of women, which included lengthy interviews dealing with a variety of topics on marital and sexual relations, attitudes between the sexes, contraception, and beliefs about fertility. This study, by J. M. Stycos (1955), isolated a number of conditions that were relevant to family planning, including that: religious beliefs did not influence women particularly on family planning, but the organizational strength of the church made establishment of a contraceptive service difficult; men did not want particularly large families, but lack of communication between partners led to misperception; similar difficulties inhibited the use of specific contraceptives. The study concentrated on a small number of respondents, with whom interviewers spent about four hours in an almost conversational setting. This approach still recognized the sensitivity of the topic and treated family planning as a purely personal problem.

The Stycos study was replicated by Judith Blake in Jamaica with substantially the same results, modified by cultural conditions, especially the open acceptance of some forms of cohabitation (Blake 1961). The successful completion of these two studies led to the next steps, which laid the groundwork for social action. A complex study, started in 1953 by R. Hill, J. M. Stycos, and K. W. Back, included a survey that measured the importance of the different conditions and translated them into applicable terms and a field experiment that included features of possible programs promoting family planning. This design threatened to be more expensive than Puerto Rican resources would permit. Here was a place where the newly expressed interest in dealing with population could become active. Conventional foundations turned down the proposal with regret, seeing it as falling still outside of acceptable social research. But the Population Council had just started to sponsor relevant research and some demographers who had not been willing to support such a study in a place like the Carnegie Corporation (whose funds were targeted toward research promoting general human welfare) were amenable to doing so under the auspices of this new organization. Even here some questions remained, but the council was willing to support a large-scale study on a population sample that would approximate the population as closely as possible.

The study included sensitive questions on sexual and contraceptive behavior and was administered mainly in a precoded interview; no intimate rapport could be established as the interviews did not take much more than an hour and frequently less; the questions were exactly predetermined and short, definite answers were required. In spite of these restrictions, cooperation of respondents, male as well as female, was secured. In addition to the substantive importance of the data the results of the interviewing showed that topics could be treated like any other public issue (Hill, Stycos, and Back 1959). Reports from this study encouraged other groups to initiate large-scale studies. A conference at the Millbank Memorial Fund developed plans for a set of research enterprises within the United States with support from various sources (Millbank Memorial Fund 1955). The results of these studies were reported in professional publications and soon in the popular press. Facts and trends in family planning soon became public knowledge; variations in family planning looked acceptable at the same time when overpopulation, at least abroad, was seen to be a matter of public concern.

Understanding can lead to intervention. When the social conditions for effective family planning could be listed and their relationships analyzed, it became possible to study public policy alternatives, such as different methods of encouraging birth control use. Here the dividing lines between research, education, and propaganda came into play, with the question raised of how far different organizations could legitimately support such studies. Another problem arose from the opposite direction. Researchers found natural allies in the planned parenthood groups, but the representatives of these organizations were unwilling to invest time and effort in purely scientific studies, rather than in programs that would be maximally effective, even if not perfectly documented and controlled.

The progress in action research can be seen in the further history of these Caribbean studies. The Puerto Rican research identified three conditions that were necessary for an individual to be successful in family planning: motivation for reducing or spacing childbirth, family situation conducive to family planning, and information about contraception. The experimental part of the study in Puerto Rico and later in Jamaica tested the importance of these conditions by systematically varying them through educational programs, either singly or in combination, and observing the effect on family planning (Hill, Stycos, and Back 1959, Stycos and Back 1965). The programs used in these experiments could then be translated into public policy. Each of these steps extends social influence beyond the goal of facilitating personal decisions and thus induces researchers to take a definite position. Should research be connected with specific types of family planning? Should research be directed to influence family size goals? Should research stick to a pure presentation of conditions, or can this scientific stance be overridden by immediate needs for service? When does research become an adjunct to a particular policy? Who decides on the policy?

That these questions were being asked indicates that the movement had entered a new stage of development. After trying to eliminate all restraints in the field, the goals of the movement became more positive; but commitment to a goal of family formation and population size implied also a willingness to fight for its accomplishment and to reject opposing views.

The Puerto Rican study answered the questions of procedure in a relatively neutral way. The design of the experiment restricted the educational efforts to the three conditions that had been isolated and added one arm to the study that combined all three topics. But the conditions were restricted to the prescriptions of the design, introducing combinations of topics and means of introducing them, like so many chemicals administered to obtain a certain reaction. There was little interest in using the information gathered to increase family planning in the country; the interest was in statistical significance rather than in meaningful effects on family planning practices. (Of course, all the educational techniques tested tended to increase the likelihood of effective family planning; neutrality did not go so far as to test methods of hindering family planning.)

The emphasis on research made it possible for a variety of agencies to fund these studies. As experiments in educational techniques they could be justified under many headings; strictly speaking, the experiments concerned technical problems such as ability to separate the different stimulus conditions or to assure that these controlled conditions could lead to measurable changes in families. The Population Council itself, which was interested in furthering population control, was willing to support research that looked academically sound and would not have local repercussions. On the other hand, the certainty that the experiments would have only limited effects lost them the support of local family planning organizations, who thought that so much effort should not be expended on work that would not have direct effects on family planning. The representatives of the family planning movement were mainly concerned with protecting their achievement of having clinical work legally and socially accepted. They could not jeopardize their hard won gains in favor of research that would lead to planning a different approach.

The insights derived from the Puerto Rican study were tested in the subsequent study in Jamaica, which was more action-oriented. Here also new sources of support were needed. The main sponsor was the Conservation Foundation, which looked at human population expansion as a possible threat to the conservation of natural resources. It had financed the study by Judith Blake on cultural conditions influencing fertility in Jamaica, and was now willing to go further than this theoretical study. There were, however, limits beyond which the foundation could not go and that included direct identification with family planning groups. On the other hand, its work included activities directed to further action on conservation and thus it was within its tradition to promote social change, even without research. Some officials were reluctant to commit the foundation to this field, but the dedication of one vice-president, Robert G. Snyder, carried the day. The foundation decided to support the basic core of a replication and extension of the Puerto Rican research.

The financing of the study demonstrates on a small scale the varying goals of organizations in the field. The Population Council supported some of the research as an extension of the Puerto Rican model. As Jamaica was then a British colony, funds were also sought in Britain. The British Colonial Office could commit development funds, but those could only be used for research (that is, a survey) but not for any educational or action purposes. But, partly through their mediation, a private foundation, the Nuffield Foundation, gave funds that could be earmarked for action. Finally, the whole project had to have local sponsorship in Jamaica, and a local group was organized to act as a sponsor for the study, the Jamaica Population Research Foundation; its board included representatives of all political and civic groups of the country, including a representative of the Catholic bishop. The study itself was conducted by J. M. Stycos and K. W. Back, based on their Puerto Rican experience.

Surviving this precarious combination, the study developed plans for effective programs rather than just comparing results of various isolated conditions. Since the results of the previous work showed that the particular topic was shown not to be very important, the educational programs could be designed for maximum effectiveness, and motivational and informational topics concerned with family planning were included in each arm of the design. The important variable in the study was the kind of educational approach used, namely group meetings, case work, and distribution of pamphlets; an additional program included all three, aiming for maximum effect. The previous studies had shown that participation in an interview could, for some individuals, make family planning sufficiently salient to induce them to practice it: different control conditions were added to measure this preinterview effect, adding a new, minimal, influence condition (Stycos and Back 1965).

The study was directed toward practical effectiveness, although the research aim was still the extraction of general principles. Cooperation with the local family planning association was possible, and participants in the study were encouraged to seek help in local clinics. Effects of the program were immediately far-reaching and decrease of fertility in the study areas persisted after more than two years (Farley and Leavitt 1968).

The conduct of the study and construction of the educational material it used explored the ways in which increased knowledge could be converted to action, hence changing the status of family planning in society. For example, a film was created to be shown at the group meetings. There were no existing films specifically addressing family planning and there still are hardly any. If the topic is approached at all it is within a general framework of social improvement or in recommending contraceptive methods as protection against venereal disease (as in U.S. Army films). In the Puerto Rican study a film produced by the National Institute of Mental Health was used; this film, in Spanish, treated all aspects of maturity in personal development, and included under this heading personal responsibility in intercourse, denouncing as immature the desire of having as many children as possible. This was as far as a U.S. government agency could go. For the Jamaican study a special film was commissioned that dealt exclusively with family planning, comparing the fate of two couples, who exemplified planned and unplanned families. It was frankly a propaganda film that used a variety of emotional techniques to achieve maximum effect. In this case it could hardly be claimed that the audience was offered only choices to achieve personal aims. In the end the film aroused controversy among sponsors, although not among the general population, and led to the resignation of Catholic representatives from the Jamaican sponsoring organization.

The precedent for promoting family planning and using the research component mainly for evaluation of the program had been established, however. In the late 1950s the Population Council established cooperation with agencies in India and Pakistan for establishing field studies. These studies showed the effectiveness of case work by indigenous workers (Population Council 1978). A little later, in 1962, the council started a long-standing cooperation with government agencies in Taiwan; at first a two-year field study under the direction of Ronald Freedman, in cooperation with the University of Michigan, consisted of saturation of some areas by an intensive mass media campaign (Freedman and Takeshita 1969). This study proved to be very successful in the sense that impact and change in family planning could be shown. The council continued its work in Taiwan, under the leadership of Bernard Berelson, who later became president of the Population Council. In 1968 Taiwan adopted an official policy in favor of population planning.

Research had become evaluation, which led later to establishment of new policies: when it had been established that educational programs were feasible and effective, it became legitimate to conduct pilot programs and to evaluate their effectiveness, no longer having to justify the promotion of family planning itself. From this it was only a small step to active promotion of family planning and the search for effective incentives for compliance.

New Sources of Support

The expansion of a limited definition of research from improvement of knowledge to service for active programs was not simply an intellectual exercise, but became important for the kind of sponsorship that family planning could obtain. In turn, any expansion of sponsors made work on family planning more respectable. The first advance in this field was made by private foundations. At first only two small foundations, the Millbank Memorial Fund and the Scripps Foundation, would support work in this field; the Population Council made larger support possible and the research more visible. The studies that were based on Population Council support expanded this base in looking for more funds for additional work. Thus the Social Science Research Center at the University of Puerto Rico cooperated in the study there, and the Conservation Foundation, the Nuffield Foundation, and even the British Colonial Office supported research in Jamaica. This period saw the great increase in private foundations, because of the more rigorous application of inheritance tax laws, and more money became available for research and welfare purposes.

In almost every case the expansion followed the same pattern. First funds were restricted to innocuous research on topics related to family planning, such as demographic or biomedical studies; then the research extended to more specific conditions of family planning. Finally research and promotion of appropriate action became accepted and support for effective conduct of programs became a function of the organization. In this way the Rockefeller-financed institutions started to support population research, among these the Population Council, then the Rockefeller Brothers Fund, and finally the Rockefeller Foundation itself. Eventually the Rockefeller Foundation established a population research program with field offices in many regions of the world. Other foundations even appeared that had as their principal aim the furtherance of family planning—for example, Clarence Gamble's Pathfinder Fund. And, Hugh Moore, who had established the Moore Fund for the promotion of peace before World War II, in the 1950s turned the fund into an aggressive advocate of family planning.

But the most influential of the new recruits was the Ford Foundation. It became active in the late 1940s and its initial program was directed toward fundamental research in the behavioral sciences. With the spirit of the times the foundation oriented itself more and more toward specific problems, and population control was a very appealing one. By the late fifties the Ford Foundation gave grants to the Population Council. But these were intended strictly for demographic research and the council adhered to this limit, partly because some of members of the Ford family were Roman Catholics. This situation soon changed, however. The foundation soon gave larger grants for wider fields of work in family planning and, even more important, entered the field with its own staff. Changes in the foundation itself directed it more toward social intervention; further, the influence of the Ford family declined, leaving the new leadership free to enter actively into many fields. Changes in the top administration led to corresponding changes of emphasis on different social actions, but the Ford Foundation had established for itself the principle that support for public action furthering family planning fell within its mission of improving knowledge and welfare. The foundation established its own demographic division. Under the leadership of the economist Oscar Harkavy and the joint efforts of Reuben Hill and the sociologist Irwin T. Sanders this division became a strong force for worldwide population planning in the late 1960s (Caldwell and Caldwell 1986).

The Ford Foundation was by far the largest private foundation; it organized itself almost like a miniature government. It maintained missions in several countries to support its programs, sent delegations to other countries to start new ventures, and approached government leaders practically on a basis of equality. But, as it did not represent directly the American government, it could act strongly, using economic planners as well as medical personnel for its purposes. Its lasting contribution was the establishment of population centers that carried on research, service, and evaluation. The Ford Foundation succeeded in helping the initiation of several programs, especially in smaller countries, such as Egypt and Kenya. But even here in these limited cases the resources needed for national programs exceeded the efforts that a private foundation could muster. It became clear that if family planning were to become more than a personal option, then public support would have to be involved.

Government Action

The involvement of governments on behalf of family planning effected a change in the attitude of the movement. The whole previous course of the movement had been in fighting government intervention and reserving an area for individual autonomy in decisions on contraception and family planning. Moreover, the topic was extremely controversial; emotional appeals could be launched from all sides and the effects of such appeals on political action seemed unpredictable. In the interest of both sides, the family planning movement as well as the public sector, separation appeared advantageous. Government officials could not be held responsible for controversial actions of the movement and the family planning movement was not subject to the vagaries of short-term change in public opinion and political manipulations.

As soon as population increase was seen as a national, even a worldwide, problem, the separation was hard to maintain. Arguments were made that the massive U.S. foreign aid effort could be undermined by excessive fertility in the receiver countries; but the sensitivities of the populations of these countries had to be taken into account as well. The government agencies concerned were careful not to promote family planning in any connection with the delivery of economic aid. In spite of this, during the 1960 presidential campaign practically all candidates made a point of attacking a (nonexisting) policy to connect the two in order to promote family planning in developing countries, because they felt sure that this was a politically advantageous stance (Gruening 1973). The domestic problem of overpopulation was, of course, not considered. As in the private sector, and perhaps as a consequence of its efforts, this situation changed in less than a decade.

The acceptance of government responsibility for population control shows the amazing effect that ideological change can have on social norms. In 1959 President Dwight Eisenhower affirmed—without much fear of public contradiction—that population control and family planning were outside the limits of governmental control, but he did that in response to a report by a government mission advocating the opposite. The network of influential persons concerned with population control was making itself felt. General William H. Draper who had been involved in some of the explorations of population problems, headed a commission that assessed the planning of foreign aid; the final report of this commission specified that all the good that foreign aid could do would be offset by excessive increase in population. This acceptance of population control in an official government document might have represented a symbolic breakthrough, had Eisenhower accepted it. Even Eisenhower's rejection brought the argument into the open. The overall situation did not change in the next few years, although President John F. Kennedy had announced during his campaign that his Catholic faith would not influence his policy in several fields, among them family planning.

With the election of 1964, President Lyndon Johnson's Great Society program created a situation similar to that of the New Deal where new programs and new government agencies were readily accepted. Senator Ernest Gruening took the lead in making family planning a government responsibility. He had been trained as physician; but rather than practicing medicine he entered various branches of government service. Under Roosevelt he had been head of a newly created Bureau of Territories and Possessions and played the role of the Washington backer in the struggle over family planning clinics in Puerto Rico. He had been elected to the Senate in 1958, representing the new state of Alaska. He now proposed the creation of two new assistant secretaries, of Health, Education and Welfare and of State, to collect and disseminate information on family planning domestically and abroad. He did not obtain as much support from his colleagues as he had hoped; only six senators cosponsored his bill initially. But in a subsequent session a somewhat weaker bill was passed, allowing for the creation of officials of lower rank and on a lower level of authority. Nevertheless, the hearings on the bill formed an important platform for the family planning movement and resulted in important documents. The initial appropriations for these new offices ranged in the hundreds of millions, much more than private foundations would have been able to spend; annual appropriation generally exceeded the capital of most foundations.

After these initial steps were taken to align family planning with government policy, this orientation soon became standard practice. Ten years after Eisenhower had denied any government responsibility for population planning, President Richard Nixon took the opposite point of view, acknowledging population control as an essential part of improvement of the quality of life without arousing any vocal opposition. He proclaimed, "One of the most serious challenges to human destiny in the last third of this century will be the growth of population. Whether man's response to that challenge will be a cause for pride or for despair in the year 2000 will depend very much on what we do today." Even more significantly, Eisenhower himself admitted that he had changed his position and that in the reconciliation of different values the benefits of family planning outweighed his objections. The principle of population control, that overpopulation was a danger and should be prevented, as well as the principle of family planning, that quality of life should be improved by controlling number and spacing of children, were now generally accepted. The tradition in international planned parenthood is to call 1965 the turning point (Suitters 1973).

Help in family planning became an integral part of the foreign aid program. The Office of Population of the Agency of International Development (AID) that administered this aid was upgraded from a branch with a corresponding budget increase. One can compare the early budget of $50 million to the potential of the largest foundations whose capital was only a fraction of this sum. The office, during its most active phase (1976–79) was headed by a physician, Dr. Ray Raventhold, who believed that the popularization of contraceptives was of the first importance (Raventhold 1968). The agency therefore sponsored an imaginative series of programs aimed at ensuring the acceptability and effective use of different kinds of contraceptives. Raventhold's emphasis was on instrumental change, rather than on changing basic attitudes toward fertility.

National Concerns

In 1969 the global population explosion had become such a visible problem that in the United States even the question of domestic overpopulation started to arouse concern, prompting Congress to establish a Commission on Population Growth and the American Future. (It was in his charge to that commission that Nixon made the statement above.) The commission, chaired by John D. Rockefeller III, held extensive hearings on all aspects of American population problems and commissioned an impressive series of research papers, completing its report in 1972. Its transmittal letter stated its main conclusion: "We have looked for, and have not found, any convincing argument for continued population growth." The commission then gave a series of recommendations to help in stabilizing population growth, including some structural changes in society, especially in the area of women's rights and family policy, and also specific aid to family planning and contraception, including abortion. In many of its recommendations the commission emphasized the need for further research and dissemination of information.

The commission had been constituted to represent a wide variety of institutions and interests and a long list of individual dissenters objected to particular recommendations. But its significance rests on the agreement on the basic principle of the aim of population stability and the furthering of family planning to reach this goal. Regardless of the specific conflicts that arose, the standards of judgment had changed: one did not have to justify any more that families should be planned and population controlled; the burden of proof fell now on showing that means not using birth control would lead to essentially the same result. On the basis of this cognitive change a new set of norms developed.

A similar change of perspective occurred in other countries as well and became a matter of international action. The United Nations from its inception had shown some interest in population questions and in 1949 a Population Division was established in the Department of Economic and Social Affairs. This division was mainly dedicated to the coordination of collection of statistics. As we have seen, this can be a first step in showing the extent of the population problem and providing firm guidelines for subsequent actions. Pressure for a more active stance, advocating aiding family planning programs, started in the mid-sixties. This was mainly carried by some European nations, such as Sweden, which had their own programs and aided other countries, and some of the South and East Asian nations, which had started their own programs and wanted United

Nations agencies to be authorized to aid them. The opposition came mainly from countries with a strong Catholic population or church influence in politics or countries whose ethnic composition was so delicately balanced that minorities felt threatened by population control. The debates on this issue became acrimonious and resulted in the usual compromise, a fact-finding project to ascertain the status of population problems in the member nations.

Accordingly the secretariat, through the Population Division, drew up a questionnaire. The terms of reference given by the UN Assembly were quite loose, and therefore, besides questions on statistics and of a general concern, questions were included that could lead to answers expressing the need for family planning. The answers by the different governments varied in emphasis, extent, and clarity; some objected to the questions and some gave general discourses on problems of demography, but a great number expressed need for some program of population control. The report on this study showed all the varying views, but documented the willingness of many countries to aid in family planning; despite opposition in some countries, it showed population expansion to be a worldwide problem that the UN could legitimately tackle (Back and Winsborough 1968–69). By this time two years had passed since the original debate. When the report was submitted, it was accepted and became the basis for a new UN activity, the United Nations Fund for Population Activities, which soon became a major force in helping to install and coordinate family planning programs.

Another outcome of the UN debate on population problems was the authorization to hold general conferences on population. These again started as information exchanges and assessment; the first conference was held in Belgrade in 1965. By the time of the second conference in Bucharest, 1974, the debate centered on the proclamation of a statement of a plan of action; specific policies and implementations were the topic of discourse. But other political considerations, such as reliance on different kinds of economic measures were introduced into the discussion and diverted attention from questions of family planning and population control (Mauldin et al. 1974). The same was true of the next conference in Mexico City, 1984. At this point, however, positions of the discussants were reversed. The developing countries pressed for aid in family planning, while the United States, the main donor country, was more concerned with avoiding support of abortion and, in general, proposed that free market economics would be as helpful (as an indirect means of population control) as direct intervention; finally a compromise agreement stressing family planning as well as economic change, was adopted (Brown 1984). Here again, in the international field, the assertion of the free flow of ideas on population control and family planning transformed the whole picture. The discussion, nationally as well as internationally, led soon to new normative concerns, this time not on ways to limit family planning and population control, but on how to further it.

Part 4

Opportunities and Challenges

Chapter Eight

Means and Ends

By the 1960s the family planning movement in the United States had in some ways achieved virtually everything that its pioneers had fought for. Both the needs of individuals for reproductive control and the problem of overpopulation were recognized as critical and discussed in the professional and popular media. Barriers against the use and provision of contraceptive methods were falling rapidly, and contraception became a standard medical prescription. Even information about the use of contraceptives was being disseminated quite freely. The freedom from constraints, which had been the target of the movement, was close at hand, even on a worldwide scale. From this success the movement could now proceed in a number of ways. It could preserve its gains, fill in some remaining deficiencies, or mark out new goals.

It cannot be said that these alternatives were faced consciously or that a sense of achievement and need for reorientation prevailed; this assessment of the situation was only made after the fact. New aims in the changing situation developed only gradually as new questions arose and new struggles presented themselves.

For instance, there were still laws on the books obstructing contraceptive practice. Two states, Connecticut and Massachusetts, prohibited the provision of contraception and contraceptive information. Since the work of private physicians was protected, this law affected only public clinics, thus serving primarily to prevent poor women from receiving contraceptive advice and service. Attempts to repeal these laws through legislation and referenda failed. But a test case on a clinic in New Haven

113

reached the Supreme Court in 1965 (*Griswold v. Connecticut*), and the court decided that any interference with a woman's right to medical care was unconstitutional. In 1970 Congress rewrote the Comstock Act, excluding contraception from its provisions. This outlawing of legal barriers against medical contraception was quickly transformed into positive action, legislation that integrated family planning into the governmental structure.

The inclusion of family planning into the Great Society programs aligned its advocates with the coalition that supported these reforms. Accordingly, opposition to family planning was sometimes included in general opposition to other reforms. In this way family planning became involved in ideological and partisan politics. The family planning movement had, of course, been frequently a partner in general political developments. The drive against censorship had helped to free contraceptive information from the Comstock Act, and the New Deal expansion of government in the social sphere had transformed government from a constant threat into a sometime partner. Only since the late 1960s, however, did issues related to family planning become central questions in political discussion and did the family planning movement find a place among an array of organizations.

New Contraceptive Methods

The achievement of the movement's general goals opened up an array of new possibilities. While contraception as such was generally accepted, the role of specific methods still had to be worked out. Although there had been little advance in new methods during the history of the movement, advances in biology and biotechnology had opened the way to completely new technologies. It was hoped that new methods, besides their practical advantages, might also bypass the moral and religious objections that adhered to traditional methods. On the other hand, some methods that had been known for a long time were still not widely acceptable contraception; the principal example here is abortion, and to a lesser degree sterilization. With the general acceptance of the aims of population control and the official sanction of contraception, the conflicts that the movement faced centered around the methods to be used. Debates about methods of contraception created new allies and opponents.

The birth control methods that were known in 1930 were of rather ancient origin, but they worked reasonably well. Hence the efforts of early work in family planning were more directed toward facilitation of using what was already available than toward finding new means of contraception. But with increased and publicized use the search for safer, more effective, and more convenient contraceptives intensified. This was not just a search for technical perfection for its own sake: while the purpose of family planning was becoming more and more accepted, opposition centered on contraception itself, either on particular techniques or on the concept. Even the Catholic church, the traditional foe of family planning, spoke favorably of responsible parenthood, but attacked "artificial" methods to achieve it. Innovators hoped that new methods would counter these objections to birth control. For example, advocating contraception had always been difficult because of the sensitive associations surrounding the sexual act. It was hoped that the farther the practice of birth control was removed from intercourse, the more acceptable it would become, both institutionally and in personal practice.

One old way used to achieve this separation was the rhythm method, which restricts intercourse to the infertile days during the menstrual cycle. This method was systematized by Catholic scientists and accepted by the church as "natural" in the 1930s. It depends on determining the timing of ovulation from the menstrual period and, using only this indicator, was only approximately accurate. The rhythm method was accepted by planned parenthood organizations for use in countries where cost and lack of hygiene argued against the use of other methods, and also in Catholic countries, where it was accepted by the church. But because of its unreliability, the rhythm method was generally not the method of choice elsewhere. Later more accurate techniques—including measurement of temperature and chemical tests—made the so-called natural methods more effective; however, since the new techniques demanded skilled record keeping and the use of some instruments, this more sophisticated rhythm method was not useful in primitive conditions. Today the method's role is primarily among families who object to other techniques for religious reasons or because of the side effects of other methods. Under these conditions, natural family planning has had a renaissance in recent years, through the Billings method (Billings and Westmore 1980), which because of improved physiological knowledge of the reproductive process and its measurement, is reliable and comparatively easy to use; it is becoming important in foreign aid programs (Hermann et al. 1986). It is also a method that depends on joint planning of the partners and is therefore congenial to couples who stress joint responsibility.

Another way of separating contraception from intercourse is the use of biochemical or biophysical means that make a woman unable to conceive for an extended period of time. (Similar efforts have been made to develop male contraceptives; but they have been mainly unsuccessful thus far.)

An early attempt of this sort was a partly physical, partly chemical device, the Lippes Loop. The first of many intrauterine devices (IUDs), it was a copper coil designed to be inserted into the uterus, which would then reject any embryo implant (Reed 1978). The Lippes Loop was developed in the 1930s in Hungary and tried by some physicians in New York. It was received with great reservations, partly because its biological rationale was not clear and partly because accidents could occur during the insertion of the loop. The loop practically vanished in the United States, but in following decades spread to the Far East through the migration of some European physicians during the war years. After the war the loop was introduced again into the United States and this time it was welcomed. Interest in improvement in contraception was increasing and the openness of the discussion made dissemination easier and production of contraceptives a lucrative commercial venture. The restrictions that had made Margaret Sanger's clinical work so difficult had been lifted.

Within a few years a number of new IUDs were designed and hailed as a great advance in contraception. Long-lasting and effective, yet quite easy to remove when desired, for a while they seemed the ideal. Eventually, however, the IUDs showed grave side effects justifying the early criticisms of the device. One of the devices, the Dalkon Shield, became the target of more than two million potential claimants in one of the largest mass damage suits in history. Fearing similar suits, other companies ceased producing IUDs. By 1986 the manufacture of the three devices that accounted for 97 percent of all IUDs sold in the United States was stopped and no new manufacture can be expected because of the threat of damage payments. It is estimated, however, that more than two million American women still want to use IUDs (Forrest 1986, Ramirez and Starrs 1987). It is still one of the most frequently used means of contraception in many countries and also an object of intense medical research (Zatuchni, Goldsmith, and Sciarra 1985), which may give a new life to this technique even in the U.S.

The ideal contraceptive mechanism for which family planning advocates were looking was a drug, preferably a pill, which could be taken daily or less often. Advances in the study of hormones led to a better understanding of the biochemical process of impregnation, which in turn led to the discovery of drugs that could interrupt the process. Following the basic scientific discovery, achieving the technical solution required a large investment of money. Since the federal government did not regard contraception as a health problem nor as an object for government concern (unlike polio for which the federal government sponsored vaccine research), the development of oral contraceptives was left in the hands of private drug companies, with some help from foundations. An oral contraceptive was designed in the late 1950s by Dr. Gregory Pincus and Dr. John Rock, with the financial help of the C. D. Searle company. Pincus did the biological research at the Worcester Foundation and Rock the clinical work in Boston.

Pincus's principal mission at the Worcester Foundation was to develop drugs regulating hormone production, principally for contraception. But Searle, the drug manufacturer that supported much of the research needed marketable products in the interim whose development costs could be recouped in subsequent sales. Some of the projects that Pincus had undertaken were scientifically valuable but none resulted in profitable products, and by 1951 Searle was understandably reluctant to invest any more large sums. Thus Pincus had to undertake his crucial research on quite a small grant. Finances were further strained because the raw source of the chemicals he needed was controlled by a Mexican government monopoly that kept the price exceedingly high. Pincus was unable to proceed until Congressional trade and antimonopoly legislation forced the price down and made it possible for him to obtain enough material for research and trials. Securing financial support was not the only difficulty the oral contraceptive project faced, in spite of wide agreement that a birth control pill would resolve many personal and social problems. One problem was the position of John Rock himself, a practicing Catholic who insisted that he could keep his religious convictions and his professional life separate. He had been for a long time a proponent of family planning, while giving full weight to ethical and religious considerations. His 1949 book, *Voluntary Parenthood,* advocated family planning, while setting forth the ethical significance of the means in each religious tradition.

Rock hoped that an oral contraceptive would be considered a "natural" rather than "artificial" means by the Catholic church and thus escape conflict (Rock 1963). His position, however, exposed him to attacks from all sides. Margaret Sanger and her associates distrusted him for being a Catholic, while Catholic groups criticized his being involved in such work at all; the medical profession, too, was skeptical of the chances of this research.

Pincus and Rock persisted despite their difficulties, however, and the result of their labor was a compound that under the trade name Enovid became the first widely marketed oral contraceptive.

The introduction of the birth control pill in 1960 can be seen as the climax of the family planning movement. Family planning was generally accepted, and reliable, easy-to-use means were now widely available. Many observers and proponents of the movement saw in the pill reason for optimism; thus James Reed's important history of the movement, *From Private Vice to Public Virtue,* considers the pill's discovery a fitting point to end the tale. Similarly, supporters hoped that a Catholic church that just had convened its council under the aegis of *aggiornamento* (modernization) in 1963 could accept oral contraceptives. The optimism was, however, not fully justified by events. Unfolding developments quickly showed that purely instrumental advances could not assure the eventual success of the movement.

New Questions

The hope that regular use of a pill, completely separated from intercourse, would not be considered an artificial contraceptive was not fulfilled. Advocates of the pill had hoped that this induced temporary infertility could be accepted in the same way as restriction of intercourse to naturally infertile days in the rhythm method. The doctrine of the church, however, perhaps due to the succession of a more conservative pope, Paul VI, in 1963, proved inflexible. The pope ordered the preparation of a new encyclical on family life and when it was issued (*Humanae vitae* 1969), it reaffirmed the church's opposition to all technical contraceptive methods. This rigid stance—which probably hurt the church almost as much as the family planning movement—served to perpetuate the strong opposition between the two.

Some obstacles to the use of oral contraceptives also arose from incomplete knowledge of the method. While the functioning of barrier methods, such as the condom, diaphragm, and jellies is readily understood, biochemical methods affect the whole body in a way that is not easily comprehensible, even to experts. Thus it is natural to fear that biochemical methods may have effects that are not easily perceived. Furthermore there is a risk that oral contraceptives may have a cumulative effect; a woman may use them for thirty years or more with deleterious effects only becoming noticeable after a few decades. Thus the exact influences of the pill cannot be predicted with certainty.

Regulatory agencies have responded to this potential risk by restricting use of these drugs to only half the time for which clinical experience has shown them to be safe for continuous use. For instance, if test groups had shown a contraceptive pill to be safe for ten years, then it was recommended for five years' use. On the one hand, this procedure resulted in a slow release of the drugs; but on the other hand it put the first cohorts to use the pill at some risk. Further the drugs might be dangerous for only some people, as has been indicated in the case of women with heart disease or who smoke heavily; these groups would not be identified by tests conducted on the whole population. If agency approval had been withheld until the original tests over a full life-span were completed and all specially sensitive groups were identified, then oral contraceptives would not have been available until the twenty-first century. As waiting that long seemed unreasonable, and the demand for immediate use was big, the contraceptives that were released by regulatory agencies were prescribed by physicians, who might have been uneasy themselves. Most doctors prescribing the pill observed their patients closely and noted any side effects.

Because the borderline between clinical and experimental use of contraceptives was not clear, it is not surprising that some of the early patients felt as if they were experimented upon. Unfortunately for the proponents of the pill the incipient women's movement used this situation as an opportunity for vehement protest. At an open meeting of the New York Academy of Sciences in the early 1970s, which discussed new developments in contraception, a group of feminists in the audience almost disrupted the meeting by staging a demonstration against the use of women as guinea pigs for furthering the work of male scientists and doctors. The demonstration was partly organized to gain publicity for the new movement, but it pointed to a real conflict between former allies. For the original pioneers one of the main virtues of family planning was freeing women from the burden of continuous pregnancy and childbearing, thus enabling them to perform new roles in society. Many of the founders of the family planning movement had also been feminists, and in turn the revival of the feminist movement was in part propelled by the effects of family planning. Now, however, the new processes of contraception were denounced as male exploitation of women. The possible dangers of the new techniques revealed an area where the interests of family planning conflicted with the interests of women. Thus while the consensus on the dangers of overpopulation and the creation of effective, available means of contraception marked a successful stage in the movement, it also brought new problems in its wake. The scientists, manufacturers, and regulatory agencies faced an uncomfortable dilemma: if they held back wide distribution until the drug was proven completely safe, they condemned generations of women to unwanted pregnancies or at least to inferior means of contraception; if they released the drug hurriedly, they might be accused of unwarranted experimentation, especially if negative effects were found later.

The Abortion Controversy

It was not only the new scientific developments that expanded the discussion on contraceptive methods. The increasing openness of discourse on sexual matters starting in the 1950s brought previously taboo topics into public discussion, including the most controversial topic of all, abortion. Abortion represented the ultimate point of opportunity and the ultimate danger for the movement, especially in its political consequences.

On a worldwide basis, abortion may well be the most widely used contraceptive method; it is, however, rarely looked upon as a method of choice. Indeed, its legitimacy is often questioned. This was not always the case. For centuries it had been Western tradition, because the Catholic church held the movement of the fetus (known as "quickening") as the criterion of the individual human soul: before it occurred, abortion was considered ethical, but afterward it was child murder. In the early nineteenth century, motivated both by better biological understanding and also by concern for the health of the mother, both secular and religious authorities initiated more rigorous sanctions against abortion at any stage of pregnancy: any induced loss of the fetus became the concern of the courts and the confessional. Given the lack of hygienic precautions, the risk of the operation was certainly considerable and thus the decision was increasingly given to physicians, who were trained in assessing health risks. Women who either could not afford or were not able to convince physicians to perform abortions were reduced to the use of questionable practitioners or primitive self-induced methods (Luker 1984).

With the general liberalization of attitudes toward issues related to sexuality in the second half of the twentieth century, physicians became more permissive, accepting psychological and economic reasons for abortion in addition to purely medical ones. What remained, however, was the woman's dependence on the physician's authority and the rigidity of the abortion laws of some states. An extremely poignant incident, the

thalidomide case, brought national attention to this situation. Thalidomide, a tranquilizing drug, had been prescribed extensively in the 1950s
for pregnant women. It turned out, however, that it had extremely dam-
aging effects on the fetus, resulting in loss or deformation of arms and
legs. In 1962 Mrs. Sheri Finkbine, a mother of four children, had taken
a strong dose of the drug during her fifth pregnancy and found that she
was at high risk for a seriously deformed child. The local hospital refused
to have the abortion performed and she petitioned the courts in her home
state, Arizona, to override the hospital authorities. This situation caught
the popular imagination and was widely featured in all media. Mrs. Finkbine was disturbed by the media attention, withdrew her petition to the
court, and went to Sweden, where the abortion was performed, after
being approved by a medical panel. This incident brought to the fore the
necessity of abortion for other than purely medical reasons: the fetus
was viable and the physical health of the mother would not have been at
stake. The plight of the parents aroused national compassion and became
a crucial focus for the liberalization of abortion laws.

Abortion as A Political Issue

The struggle over abortion fits into the pattern of previous experiences
of the family planning movement. Civic pressure groups tried to influence
legislators to introduce and support proabortion laws—predominantly at
the state level, for it was unlikely that federal legislation would pass. At
the same time a parallel effort was mounted on the judiciary front in
identifying the right to abortion as a civil rights issue. Following the earlier pattern, the course of the struggle was helped by a change in the
moral climate that speeded up the process. On the other hand, the nature
of the issue was different and unique: abortion aroused special opposition, and even its proponents could readily accept some limitations.

At first changes in laws were achieved in some states, notably California, Colorado, and, in 1970, New York. Abortion occurs rarely in any
woman's life; in contrast to most other contraceptive methods, it does
not have to be continually present to be available when needed. Thus the
presence of a few centers where abortion was legal gave many women
access to it. In some states, such as New York, no proof of residence
was required. Therefore, legalization of abortion by individual states had
a limited national effect, since abortion was available to any woman who
could afford to travel to those states. Action by Congress was unlikely,
given the experience of previous family planning bills. The efforts of the

family planning movement were directed therefore toward court actions. The Supreme Court had ruled in favor of family planning in several instances, most notably outlawing any state restrictions of public family planning clinics and in recognizing the same right of the unmarried as of the married to contraception (*Eisenstadt v. Baird,* 1972). Supreme Court decisions in other cases generally upheld the protection of the privacy of the patient and the protection of the right of physicians to act in the interests of their patients' health, overriding particular social norms. It was felt that the same argument could be applied to abortion, if the same judicial majority would act consistently according to these principles. It was a long time before the court accepted a test case; but in 1973 the Court found in *Roe v. Wade* that states could not interfere with the privacy of the woman nor the professional duty of the physician. It thus declared all state laws outlawing abortion to be unconstitutional, affirming that the fetus was not a person having constitutional protection (Barnett 1982). The Court, however, accepted some interests of the state in regulating abortion; many of these were not spelled out, leading to continuing litigation about specific acts of legislatures. The decision emphasized the crucial importance of viability, the ability of the fetus to live outside the womb. In the decision, viability was roughly measured by the stage of the pregnancy. In the first three months medical judgment could prevail absolutely; in the second, the state could place some restrictions on medical practice; in the third trimester the state could regulate and even proscribe abortion. Thus, the Court ruled that if the fetus was viable, its own status in law must be considered. With these provisos, however, advocates of abortion seemed to have won a decisive victory.

Nevertheless, this victory did not establish a clear-cut legitimacy for abortion. In contrast to other methods, abortion is rarely advocated as a contraceptive technique for general use. Even in the arguments of its proponents, it is generally defended as an action of last resort, when other methods have failed or were not used. (In fact, a reaction of the Planned Parenthood Federation to the arguments against abortion has been to advocate greater support for other contraceptive techniques, which would obviate the use of abortion.) In other words, while there are many proponents of the right to abortion, there are few proponents of its use.

Thus, abortion presents a clear target for its opponents. The borderline between abortion and infanticide is sometimes hard to draw; even the crucial Supreme Court decision left the determination in the last months before birth to state regulation. Advances in medicine will extend the limits of viability. Opponents of abortion can easily argue the arbitrary nature of this dividing line and make a strong appeal for the rights of the fetus. Again this is easier to do because most proponents of the right to abortion set limits on its use; the reservations involved in advocacy of the right to abortion gave in effect an opening to opponents of the family planning movement. Complete opposition at least has the virtue of consistency.

Abortion opponents have a clear point of attack, while its defenders have to use complicated rhetoric. This dilemma is reflected in public opinion on the issue. There are few other topics where the design of survey questions makes so much difference in the outcome of public opinion research. Most studies on this topic list attitudes toward different reasons for abortion; the range between acceptance of abortion when life of the mother is at stake and its acceptance when only questions of lifestyle are involved is considerable. In most studies the first leads to practically unanimous acceptance of abortion, while in the second case fewer than half the respondents accept it. Thus one can say that abortion in critical cases is well accepted while abortion on demand is still a controversial topic.

Historical conditions led to the prominence of abortion and made it a symbolic issue in many political and ideological fields. Ironically, the abortion struggle with its mixed results gave the family planning movement a public prominence that it had not been able to achieve despite all its successes during the past century.

The Right-To-Life Movement

The abortion issue accentuated the question of life-style in the United States, a problem that had grown during the 1960s. The slogan against George McGovern's campaign for president in 1972, that it was run on a platform of "abortion, acid, and amnesty [for draft evaders]" shows a vaguely felt opposition against a number of social trends. Here we find again the unrest and social excitement that may lead to the start of a social movement. The abortion decision became the precipitating event that did create such a movement.

The right-to-life movement can be seen as a negative image of the early stages of the family planning movement. Where the family planning movement derived its impetus from trying to remove restrictions, the right-to-life movement started by opposing relaxations and advocating new limits on birth control practice. The family planning movement had an array of goals and was frequently an offshoot of other trends in society, such as English radicalism, anarchism, the women's or civil rights movements. The right-to-life movement focused intently on one issue, outlawing abortion, and had strong internal conflicts over allying itself with any other issues (Spitzer 1987). The family planning movement was, especially at the beginning, led by strong individuals, who became its heroes and heroines; there are hardly any figures who have achieved prominence as activists in the right-to-life movement. This contrast is even more remarkable because of another distinctive feature. The family planning movement, because of its links with other issues, did not make its aims an electoral issue; the right-to-life movement very quickly organized itself as a political party and run candidates for political office, even the presidency (in 1980 it received thirty-two thousand votes). In spite of this exposure, the leaders of the movement, even including its presidential candidate, Ellen MacCormack, are quite anonymous. Correspondingly it is quite difficult to trace the origin of the movement to any specific activities. Studies of the active members of the movement typically reveal people who were concerned and then contacted an existing organization in the community. Mrs. MacCormack had only local and community experience before starting the National Right-to-Life Committee in her living room. The right-to-life movement looks like a model of a grassroots movement, with all its strength and weaknesses.

The earliest strength of the movement was shown in California and New York, the states in which the strongest abortion reform legislation was passed, indicating that the movement was started by coalescing the relatively uncoordinated groups that had opposed abortion in the state legislatures and later in the court cases. The New York Right-to-Life Party entered its candidates for the first time in 1970, after the relaxed abortion law was passed. Testimony against relaxation came mainly from representatives of Catholic organizations who then continued in their communities their work in front of the legislature. The first support for an organized right-to-life movement came from the Catholic church. The financial support in the first years, the early 1970s, in New York as well as in other states, came from the funds of a number of dioceses. This is not to say that the church actively went out to organize the movement; the records of early active members show that they themselves actively sought out support for their views. The reports of interviews give a picture of women who were outraged by the action of proabortion groups, sometimes because of their own experiences of miscarriage or stillbirth (Luker 1984). The typical recruit was a suburban housewife who would contact a group whose address was already listed in the telephone directory, devote some of her time to the movement, soon becoming an active worker. In this way the campaign acquired its strength. The origin of the available addresses and telephone numbers came typically from equally informal sources. Thus the origin of the National Right-to-Life Committee came from a discussion in the home of Mrs. MacCormack who had had minor experience in local politics. It is true, however, that these first groups consisted mainly of Catholics, who had a strong religious commitment against abortions and, indeed, against contraception. Their general outrage against current moral conditions found here an effective outlet.

The aim of these right-to-life groups was very specific: at first, opposition against the liberalization of laws, then against the court decisions, and finally against the various implementations and additions to these landmarks, such as the financial support of abortion. The movement was successful in the latter struggles.

The social reforms of the sixties had included some public financing of the medical costs of abortion, particularly in the Medicare and Medicaid programs. In the 1970s the question was whether these programs should pay for abortion and under what conditions they should do so. Up to 1977 Congress did not put any restrictions on Medicaid, but in 1977 it passed the Hyde Amendment, which prohibited the use of Medicaid for abortions unless the life of the mother was in danger. This issue went to the courts, and later that year the Supreme Court in two decisions (*Maher v. Doe* and *Beal v. Roe*) acknowledged the right of Congress to deny funds for nontherapeutic abortions. Individual states, however, do provide funds for abortion services, and the debate about the appropriations regularly brings prolife and proabortion forces to the fore.

The debate about the use of public funds reveals again the peculiar legal status of abortion. The strongest argument of abortion rights' advocates, and the one implicitly adopted in *Roe v. Wade*, is that abortion is a recognized medical procedure and therefore a protected private matter between doctor and patient. But in this case Congress would have the right to list or exclude the use of public funds for any nonmedically necessary operation, such as cosmetic operations or sterilization. Although this is different from interfering with the use of abortion in the medical process itself, the 1977 decisions made it difficult for poorer women to obtain abortions, as for other medical procedures in the same category. But here the proponents of abortion use civil rights arguments to assert that women have a right to abortion and that the state is constitutionally obliged to provide funds to exert this right. This argument makes abortion different from other operations and puts it into the public domain, exposing it to political and legal control. This special status had been acknowledged in the *Roe v. Wade* decision, which took into account the rights of a viable fetus. Similarly, it would be questionable to force Catholic hospitals under Catholic control to perform abortions or else lose public support or even be guilty of malpractice, as could be done with a different kind of operation. Because of questions of this kind abortion has involved many legislative debates about seemingly unrelated issues, especially in the civil rights field.

The right-to-life movement stayed specifically concerned with one issue and used almost exclusively political means to achieve it. In this form it reached its high point around 1980 when it influenced candidates in primaries, especially for the presidency, and the party platforms themselves. As a one-issue movement, the compromises necessary for inclusion as planks in national platforms were not satisfactory and the movement launched its own electoral campaign. This also reached its peak in the 1980 election, but after this it was also clear that a party committed to just this one issue could not become a dominant force in national or even state politics. It then succumbed to the common fate of third parties in the United States. Many followers hoped to influence the major parties, especially the Republican party, while only a minority stayed committed to the one-issue party. Some extremists started to resort to violence—attacks on abortion clinics—which put that part of the movement out of the mainstream of American politics. On the other hand, the movement succeeded in incorporating its concern into the political debate of the time. As a one-issue political party, its history has been short, but in many ways its influence is still present and carried by local organizations. This short, distinct history stands in contrast to the gradual development of the family planning movement, which adapted as a diffuse cultural force to social change.

Family planning has been transformed through this period of acceptance and of new problems. In both of its branches, population control as well as contraception, the movement achieved goals that brought forth opposing reactions. While it is unlikely that we are witnessing a purely cyclical movement and that the rise of family planning will be followed by a corresponding decline, several possible paths are still open to it. One is a simple dissolution of the movement as such, with some of the changes that it has brought about becoming part of the general culture.

Another is a transformation of the movement beyond its original goals of removing social barriers to contraception and providing freedom of choice, to seeking enforceable social norms of birth control. A third choice is a continuing effort, especially in the face of countermovements, to maintain the current position and to define more sharply what the aims of the movement ought to be.

Chapter Nine

More or Less than a Movement?

In the early years of the family planning movement questions of organization absorbed a great part of the participants' efforts. Decisions had to be made and lengthy discussions were held about the priority of various possible actions, including whether to generate publications, lobby, support test cases, open clinics, and search for cooperative physicians. The issues were joined between different personalities and different groups and the outcomes determined whose leadership was accepted and what shape the movement eventually took.

In later years these debates over priorities receded. More groups joined with the specifically birth control-oriented associations for common action and different groups were formed to address only special aspects of birth control. The cause of family planning had many different aspects and could support many different activities. The structure of the movement was no longer unitary; different types of organizations could make their own contributions. Many of these allied groups and individuals accepted only some of the family planning goals. Little was left of the original conditions that led to the genesis of the family planning movement: there was no general feeling of discomfort, no feeling of powerlessness, no attraction to a new solution that would change social relationships and solve social problems. The problem of overpopulation was generally recognized and its prevention was fast becoming a social norm; the proximate means of solution—contraceptive techniques— were widely known and available, although still improvable and still controversial. Opponents of the accepted belief in the danger of over-population were now on the defensive and had to justify their views.

Of course, the current conditions were not ideal, compared to the aspirations of the founders: world population was still growing at an alarming rate and many couples did not have the number of children they wanted; even if they did, the promised rise of human happiness had not been realized. Financial support for these remaining problems could have been greater; but even more important, it also became clear that the provision of effective contraceptives, while important, solved neither population nor personal problems by itself. Many ramifications of the understanding of social, political, and legal processes, and of dealing with individual persons and their aspirations, were still to be explored. Moreover, few of these questions were amenable to direct social action. They were part of the whole political and social process to which the family planning organizations could contribute, but in which they were not distinct from other pressure groups. What we can observe here is the transformation of a dynamic social movement, after it has achieved its essential aims, into part of the establishment. One indicator of this change was that the movement was fighting for its share of public funds, which it now considered its due—a far step from its anarchistic ancestry in the beginning of the century. The organizational structures of the movement persist, but it has to change in its approach, acting as insider instead of outsider.

One new direction for the movement was a turn toward international expansion. The movement's involvement in a worldwide effort underlined the growing difference between those who wanted to participate in a struggling social movement and those who wanted to apply technical knowledge for a desired goal. Much of the family planning organization still looked back to the time when the need for fighting against the system was clear. For these groups action was more appealing than the need for comprehensive understanding of all the complex relations that go into control of population size. Many groups tried an array of simple solutions to overcome resistance—whether political, social, cultural, or individual—whatever was most traditional or comfortable for them. Others in the movement, particularly scientists, felt, however, that reliance on single approaches was incomplete and tried to develop an integrative approach. This tack gained credence and family planning and population control became seen less as a field that needed political and social activists than as one that needed scientific understanding. This was one of the consequences of the general acceptance of at least some of the aims of the movement.

We shall first consider some of the separate approaches tried by those for whom direct action was desirable and turn later to the attempts at comprehensive understanding made by those who wanted to apply technical knowledge.

The Planned Parenthood Federation of America (PPFA)

The rival factions of the American birth control movement amalgamated in 1939 into the American Birth Control Federation, which changed its name in 1942 into the Planned Parenthood Federation. The new establishment direction of the movement was signaled by the fact that the mediation was accomplished by an expert in publicity and fund raising, D. Kenneth Rose; he promoted the neutral name of planned parenthood, which would be consistent with increase as well as decrease of fertility. He also tried to separate the movement from its strong female and feminist emphasis. The name, Planned Parenthood League, which Rose finally got accepted, was opposed by the original leaders of the movement, such as Margaret Sanger. She objected to the implication that the league would also be concerned with sterility and allied problems. The league made her honorary president, recognizing her exalted position in the movement but eliminating her from active leadership; she sold her birth control clinic and the building in which it had been located to Abraham Stone, eliminating her financial stake and control. Similar exclusion happened to other former officials, such as Clarence Gamble. Stone remained active in the leadership of the federation, and also represented the United States in the international arena as its vice-president. In his position as medical leader, nationally as well as internationally, he was succeeded after his death in 1959 by Alan Guttmacher.

The postwar development of the movement also transformed the organizations. Social acceptance of birth control led to greater emphasis on service in contrast to agitation for social change. The service function had been foreshadowed in the works of the birth control clinics, such as Sanger's. But these were to a great degree seen as spearheads for innovation or as test cases to probe governmental or privately organized opposition. Now the main function of the clinics was to provide a family planning service that was not only authorized, but practically mandated by legislation. This change was shown in the growing importance of local affiliates. In 1986 the Planned Parenthood Federation had 188 affiliates in forty-two states and the District of Columbia, which were staffed by twenty thousand volunteers, besides the professional staff.

Income as well as expenditures reflected the growing importance of the affiliates' clinical service. In 1981 the whole federation had a total budget of $173 million, $149 million of which was the affiliates'. Almost one-half of this came from government grants, mainly for local services; an additional $37 million of the local income came from direct fees for service. The central office used only $25 million, $14 million of which came from government sources, mainly for its foreign program. It collected a significant amount—$9 million—from private sources; $3 million of this was allocated to the Alan Guttmacher Institute, the research arm of the movement. Thus to a great extent the Planned Parenthood Federation has become a social service organization, providing the birth control service it had promoted in its origins. It still keeps its original functions going, however; the Guttmacher Institute has a respectable research budget and provides much of the information needed for implementation of effective family planning. The Planned Parenthood Federation also maintains its capacity for independent social action if government support fails or turns into opposition. When cuts were threatened because of Planned Parenthood's provision of abortion service, it was able to mobilize its political action and oppose the Reagan administration's antiabortion stance. For a great part the federation uses its huge resources to maintain public service in its field, acting mainly to preserve its status and current activities.

As family planning has become a recognized issue in society, the promotion of new and special ideas has been assumed by other groups. To some degree family planning has become part of the agenda of other groups in related fields; thus the Sierra Club, a conservation and environmental organization, sees population control as one of its concerns. A number of other organizations provide an interlapping network of research, communication, and possible action; they range from the Population Resource Center, which is mainly supported by the Population Association of America, a professional organization of demographers, to the Center for Population Options and the World Population Society, which try to focus concern and action on population problems. In addition, a number of foundations and research organizations remain active in introducing new methods and evaluating existing programs and needs.

The array of research and informational groups is supplemented by organizations that combine personal commitment with public actions. In the 1970s particular groups sprang up in this country that tried to translate these ideas into individual actions. One of the most prominent was Zero Population Growth (ZPG), founded in 1968, which reached thirty-four thousand members in 1972 and seven hundred thousand in the 1980s; it is committed to population control in contrast to family planning. A more extreme group of this kind was NON (National Organization for Non-Parents), founded in 1971, for couples who desired no children at all, but it mainly tried to act as a support group for couples who had made this decision. These groups with largely domestic concerns were sometimes close to the burgeoning ecology movement, which looked at limiting the human population as the other side of protecting the natural environment. The general flavor of this approach is shown in the slogan The Population Explosion Is Everybody's Baby. A study of the membership in 1971 (Barnett 1974) showed a great proportion of students and upper income groups; the membership was also highly active in politics and overlapped with membership in conservationist and environmentalist organizations: 41 percent of ZPG members belonged to other such organizations. The combination of personal commitment and social action can be effective but it has the danger that the different purposes can lead to conflicts, especially if they are too diffusely spread. This uncertainty of direction was shown when a large state affiliate of ZPG California split off in 1985 because a great part of the membership wanted to become more action-oriented, such as influencing legislation. The new organization, Californians for Population Stabilization, advocates action in all appropriate fields, including immigration as well as family planning.

Other activities, which had taken much of the effort of the early movement, were taken over by specialists. One was the work on the legal aspects of family planning. Here, too, the acceptance of family planning in the general culture made it possible for established universities to devote their efforts to this problem. In the forefront are two centers established especially for this purpose at Tufts and Columbia University. Similarly, medical research in contraceptives is carried on regularly in medical schools and research universities; in addition, special research laboratories by drug firms and foundations (foremost the Population Council) continue work in this field.

Among all these organizations the Planned Parenthood Federation of America has kept a key position as the established center of continuing support for birth control. It may not respond to all the issues the movement will have to address, but as the principal private source of service and widespread organization, it represents the movement in the public eye and thus is able to speak for it.

International Organization

While the federation tried to cooperate with government in channeling funds to family planning services, new opportunities were still open for innovative action. The expanding international concern needed new organization and also new techniques to adapt to different conditions. Of course, the U.S. birth control movement had always been connected with foreign sources and the flow of influence went both ways. Pioneers like Emma Goldman and Margaret Sanger had gone to Europe in the early years of the century for relevant training and in search of new methods of contraception. In the years after World War II the population pressures in much of the world gave the American movement new justification and incentives.

Sanger had had foreign contacts for most of her career and had organized international conferences. In the postwar world she quickly saw the need and opportunity for further international action. A Japanese newspaper invited her for a lecture tour in 1949; however, the occupation authorities, represented by General Douglas MacArthur, refused her a visa for entry (Reed 1978). This refusal was mainly due to the fear that she might stir up religious and political conflict in a delicate situation, an opinion that was supported by a letter to MacArthur from Marie Stopes, Sanger's old foe. Sanger's failure in Japan contrasted with the relative success of the Rockefeller-sponsored mission and showed the virtue of an indirect, cautious approach in such circumstances. In a foreign environment undisguised advocacy of contraception, especially by outsiders, can strike sensitive nerves, related to underlying suspicion of racist motivation. The Japanese were unlikely to have forgotten the clamor about the "yellow danger." So, opposition could occur even in a country like Japan, with its activist tradition of action in birth control. The balance between indigenous movement and foreign aid became crucial in a worldwide movement.

Fortunately for further progress, native leaders appeared in several countries (Suitters 1973). Elise Ottesen-Jensen, a Swedish leader in sex education and contraception, organized an international conference in Stockholm in 1946 and from this base the International Planned Parenthood Federation (IPPF) was created. Work on the future of this venture provided an opportunity for a new start for Margaret Sanger, who had reached a personal crisis due to problems with her own health and grief over the loss of her contemporaries, as well as the changes of the birth control movement in the United States. She could invest her knowledge, experience, and enthusiasm in the international organization. She also enlisted new coworkers; with general acceptability of the movement these were usually socially prominent women who could, in addition to their own abilities, contribute funds from their families and those of their friends; the names on IPPF committees sounded like a roll call of major industries.

These efforts led to a new meeting within two years, in Cheltenham, England, in 1948. It was a large meeting, including 140 participants from seventeen countries. Although sponsored by the British Family Planning Association, its success was mainly due to Sanger's efforts and her personal recruits. Prominent among them was Dorothy Brush who herself financed the cost of maintaining a permanent central office of the federation and worked for it full-time in varying capacities. The meeting also attracted prominent persons as participants: cochairmen were Sir Boyd Orr, the Director of the UN Food and Agriculture Organization (FAO), and Lord Horder, the king's physician. The presence of such notables insured respectful media attention. Perhaps just as important was the participation of prominent demographers, among them Frank Notestein and Pascal Whelpton, who represented the interest in population control for general social reasons and cemented in this way the alliance between the two branches of the movement. Demographers had formed their own international organization, the International Union for the Scientific Study of Population; the program of their meetings regularly included sessions on fertility and even specifically on population control. These international meetings held in many cities of the world kept up the interest and visibility of the topic.

Further meetings of the IPPF were held outside of Europe, as far as possible, to arouse interest in the target countries. The next two meetings were in Bombay (1952) and in Tokyo (1955). In addition, there were regional meetings, such as a Western Hemisphere meeting in Puerto Rico (1954). These sessions had internal as well as external consequences. They allowed practitioners as well as organizers to keep in contact with each other. Through these personal relations they could keep up their morale and refresh their ideas; they also could learn about progress and experience in specific techniques. At this point the IPPF was well established and became an influential force in all discussions on pertinent issues. By 1987, the IPPF had 123 member countries. The budget had increased continually, until it reached $52 million in 1984, 88 percent from government contributions. In this year, however, the U.S. government withdrew its funding of $11 million because of the IPPF's support of abortion activities. Thus the expansion was halted, but the IPPF recovered its budget size within two years and its 1987 is estimated at close to $60 million. (These comparisons, however, are not based on constant dollars) (IPPF 1985, 1986.)

The vicissitudes of the IPPF parallel similar troubles of the PPFA; the reliance on government support for service by a socially active organization exposes it to shifts in the political climate and domestic political considerations. Both the international and the national organization have retained sufficient independence to lose government funding rather than to accept new limitations on its activities. In these crisis situations the organizations fall back on the positions and rhetoric they developed when they were fighting for recognition. Similar situations occur when developing countries change their position on population control and stop their public programs. This happened in Malaysia and the local planned parenthood organization stepped in when the government clinics stopped contraceptive service.

Private Efforts: The Pathfinder Fund

Other international organizations initiated parallel efforts. We note again Clarence Gamble who had concentrated his efforts on the Pathfinder Fund, which he had created after he had left the leadership of the Planned Parenthood Federation (Williams and Williams 1978). The Pathfinder Fund concentrated on sponsoring studies focusing on the introduction of new, presumably simple, contraceptive methods in developing societies. If Margaret Sanger represented the organizational dynamo in the field, Clarence Gamble was an example of the activist on contraceptive methods.

Gamble supported for a period work on voluntary sterilization, which had been for some time a special issue in contraceptive work. Sterilization is a relatively simple method of population control that is particularly effective because it is a single action that does not have to be repeated. This advantage, however, is also one of its greatest drawbacks: the operation is irreversible, or practically so, and the patients may be unhappy later because of changed circumstances or because they did not completely understand the meaning of the operation. Thus the influence of professionals on a patient's decision is of the greatest importance and may frequently reflect ulterior motives. Gamble himself was forced to realize this danger when he was accused of supplying his own funds to planned parenthood workers to use as incentive payments for sterilization.

Advocacy of sterilization has always had a marginal position in the family planning movement. Its most vocal advocates had been moved partly by eugenic considerations; this was true of Gamble himself. The Planned Parenthood League has rejected it. An increasingly cautious promotion of sterilization is reflected in the changes in name of the organization promoting it, from Birthright Inc. to the Human Betterment Foundation of America to the Association for Voluntary Sterilization. Although its use was, and is still very widespread, both in the United States and abroad, sterilization never became the basis for a popular movement or for international policy. Sterilization is, however, today the most popular contraceptive method in the United States. About two-fifths of contracepting couples are sterile, while the next most popular method, the contraceptive pill, is only used by one-fifth of these couples. This wide acceptance of sterilization has only occurred since the mid-sixties, however (Bumpass 1987). Gamble for one left the sterilization organization and turned to the promotion of other methods that could be used widely in overpopulated countries.

Gamble found prominent physicians in many countries with whom he was willing to cooperate. They started a number of studies, the most prominent ones in India and Japan, establishing clinics in villages, which distributed an array of contraceptive methods. The work in Japan was amazingly successful, resulting in a remarkably quick reduction in fertility in the three villages in which the clinics operated. By contrast, while the clinics in India looked like successful enterprises, the final results showed that only a minority of the women used contraception and decline in fertility was small. These results reflect general demographic conditions in both countries; Japan approaching population stability, while India's population is still increasing.

The work on enhanced international distribution of contraceptives shows a pattern of initial successes that at first looks encouraging but often reaches a plateau. In the introduction of new contraceptive methods to a community, the tapped are those who are highly motivated to prevent future pregnancies and with these recruits the enterprise succeeds. In order to reach beyond these initial recruits, however, to the less motivated the availability of easy contraceptive methods is not enough and the clinic program frequently stagnates.

Gamble hoped that simple methods could overcome reluctance toward family planning and tried to introduce more innovations in foreign communities. He had been encouraged by some attempts to use fabric saturated with saline solution as a primitive diaphragm and hoped that this could fill the need for a simple method. He was faced, however, with local objections that the American physicians were using the women in these areas simply for experiments and this resistance finally overcame the attempts to encourage family planning by these simple means.

The efforts to stress primarily the means of contraception represent one important branch of the family planning movement. Although this branch had its limitations, it worked out carefully the effects of the new techniques as they became available and made them useful for large scale work. Gamble and his coworkers recognized the importance of social factors. At the twenty-fifth anniversary of the Pathfinder Fund anniversary medals were given to almost an equal number of physicians and social researchers, recognizing the contribution of both sides. But, in effect, this branch followed the individualized, clinical aspect of the movement, introducing contraception through direct influence on the user.

The general model of clinical trials has been followed in most international aid programs up to the present. The introduction of new methods of contraception and the integration of contraceptive services into other public programs have all been tried; different kinds of medical, public health, nutrition, and pediatric care have became part of family planning programs and vice versa. Family planning has become accepted as a purely medical service in most countries. This is again a measure of the success of the movement. Family planning has become respectable, the ways of maintaining successful services can be widely discussed, improvements are important topics in scientific meetings, one can find a large number of centers for training and research in the field, and leaders are honored in many ways. Many voices from a different perspective claim, however, that the population crisis is still upon us and that additional action is needed.

The Crisis Atmosphere

While the established status of family planning could easily be looked upon as an adoption of an ideologically neutral innovation (for example, Everett Rogers [1973] has discussed family planning as a model of communication) to some degree it has remained a social issue. The sense of a social problem was reinforced in the 1950s and 60s by a series of writers who stressed the imminence of a population crisis.

Prominent among these writers were two biologists, Paul Ehrlich and Garrett Hardin. Population biology and ecology look at the relations and fate of whole species and therefore view demographic questions from the point of view of the whole human species or the future of the earth. Scientists in the field therefore view population control from a large-scale perspective and depict overwhelming forces threatening humanity. In addition, Ehrlich and Hardin had the gift of using vivid images; Ehrlich invented the term *population bomb* (1968), and Hardin *spaceship earth* (1975). Together they painted a picture of the world as a contained shell within which the inexorable force of population growth is testing the limits.

For a while books promoting these ideas became best-sellers; the threat of overpopulation became a popular idea. Science fiction and movies (the film *Soylent Green,* for instance) depicted scenarios of the future under the threat of overpopulation. Emergence of fears of this kind weakened restraints against public action in this sensitive field. Hardin urged the necessity of individual restraint by painting a vivid image in his essay "The Tragedy of the Commons" (Hardin 1970) of a village that has a grazing ground available to all householders in the community, which has ample grazing for just one cow per household. A few householders may use two cows in order to double their yields. More households follow until the common is overgrazed and all cattle starve. The message is that individual self-interest will lead to common catastrophe. But individual altruistic actions will not help. If a few households reduce their cattle for the common good, then the rest will still push to the limit and the altruists will not even have enjoyed the temporary advantage of the extra cattle. Thus the only remedy is concerted action through enforced agreement among the householders or by outside fiat.

This story is, of course, a vivid description of the Malthusian dilemma, but it points to a new solution: rather than looking to natural forces or prudent self-restraint to avert the strain on the limits of subsistence, some social coercion is seen as necessary, because one has to overcome action that may look rational for the individual. Hardin reinforced this conclusion in other images, such as a full lifeboat that cannot take additional victims out of the water without sinking. He and like-minded writers prepared the ground for public pressure and public action for population control, beyond the purely instrumental approaches of the family planners.

The immediate application of these ideas was to international aid programs, in accordance with the large-scale perspective of the writers. The argument could be made that foreign aid is detrimental, even to the recipient, if it is not accompanied by a requirement for family planning. This proposed requirement not only justified governmental action, but even justified pressure for birth control from one government upon another, an extremely sensitive issue. In a similar vein, Hardin urged that migration from high-fertility to low-fertility, industrialized, countries punishes the latter for being prudent and controlling their own fertility and then paying for the lack of restraint of the other countries. Arguments of this kind, as well as implied anti-foreign-aid stance, made Hardin's "promethean ethics" politically conservative and anathema to the usual liberal allies of the family planning movement. On the other hand, Hardin's stance in favor of abortion showed that the population crisis proponents cannot be easily classified along the conventional political spectrum.

The sensational impact of the first crisis writing may have worn off, but visible activity remains to keep the crisis atmosphere in people's minds. A world population clock in Washington shows graphically the inexorable increase of humanity and appropriate ominous events, such as the world population reaching five billion, receive wide media publicity. Concern with large-scale population problems persists as a motivating force for family planning.

Government Action

A major test of the position of a social movement is its relation to the state. The trials of the family planning movement in its early phases had been severe because of the state's opposition; since the 1960s the relation to the state had become more friendly and some support of family planning, its aims or its methods, seems to be required now of a modern government. In its publication honoring its fifteenth anniversary in 1984 the United Nations Fund for Population Problems collected statements from the leaders of 128 of its member nations who proclaimed the importance of various forms of population control activities, or at least accepted importance of the problem (UNFPA, 1985). This response stands in contrast to the situation two decades before when a UN inquiry that was less public received a low proportion of replies, many of which were evasive (Back and Winsborough 1968–69).

Official pronouncements by heads of states are of course primarily records for public consumption. The choice of bromides public leaders consider wise and politically safe to issue is significant, but the translation of these sentiments into government action is another question. Most states today are willing to concentrate on the instrumental approach, freeing contraceptive methods from restriction and supporting clinics to give birth control advice and implementation; they also will give specific goals of fertility rates to achieve by a certain date. This achievement has gone beyond the dreams of the original birth control movement, but it does not look sufficient in the crisis atmosphere that the new voices of the movement have tried to create.

Policies intended to motivate decrease in childbearing are more difficult to initiate and maintain, due to the prochild attitude that is an implicit factor in human culture and governmental policy. Practically all welfare policies are pronatalistic, in favor of fertility, including maternity benefits, child support, support for day-care, free schooling, even tax deductions for dependents. In all these tax-supported benefits the citizens who have fewer children pay for those who have more. Provision of incentives for population control or disincentives for procreation have to counteract these ingrained perspectives. Examples of actual policies can show the novel aspects of these policies. One can think of possible, even stronger methods and realize the limits that still restrain the family planning movement.

Singapore has instituted a consistent disincentive policy for large families (Fawcett and Chen 1979). It is a small country, with practically the whole population concentrated in one city on an island. The constraints on population expansion are thus easily perceptible. The population is ethnically homogeneous (more than three-quarters Chinese), but this majority is the product of relatively recent immigration. As in many migrations of this kind, men arrived first and thus the establishment of families in Singapore is more recent and offers less traditional opposition to family limitation policies than elsewhere. Politically, the country has been governed by one party practically since its inception. This party, the People's Action Party, has established an efficient bureaucracy, which administers a strong welfare system. Commentators have described it as a "stable, authoritarian political leadership espousing a strong population policy that is implemented through a respected and powerful bureaucracy to a public that is heavily dependent on government for the necessities and amenities of life" (Fawcett and Chen 1979).

The population control policies affect many areas of social policy. Maternity benefits are graded according to family size and fees are waived if the woman is sterilized after the birth of the child. In school priority is given to first or second children or those with one sterilized parent. Income tax consideration and maternity leave are not given for later children and housing preference is given to smaller families. Subsidized sterilization and abortion are available on demand. Studies have shown that these policies, especially the educational and maternity benefits, are visible enough to actually influence people's decisions. The policies are so pervasive that government officials take into account their effects on population control in planning other government actions.

Singapore's population program resulted in dramatic reductions of the fertility rate and can be seen as a standard of government action. Because of its one-party system it was able to effect its policies without political turmoil, combining motivational incentives for small families with provision of all contraceptive means available. Singapore also has an active planned parenthood association, which uses its facilities to aid the government program. The program also produced an unforeseen result. It was especially effective in the upper income groups, which were less in need of the advantages of family planning, probably because some of the incentives were most beneficial to educated women, aiding their career plans. In fact, the decline in the birth rate among the more educated families was so large that old concerns about eugenics arose and the Prime Minister appealed to university educated women not to neglect future generations. The Singapore program demonstrated that successful population control programs could reach a limit in relation to other national concerns. Few nations really want their population to decline.

Government intervention in other places encountered more serious problems. The example of India is the most striking. The family planning movement had a long history in India with strong support in the Congress Party, which assumed control of the country after independence. India's movement was host to the first non-European congress of the international family planning movement, and it produced leaders on a national and international scale. The thickly settled subcontinent also gave scope for several pioneering clinical programs that were later publicly subsidized; the Indian situation had for a long time been of special concern to the international family planning movement because of the high population density and the variety of programs attempted. It seemed a good setting for more intensive governmental efforts (Bhende and Khanikar 1982).

Large industries, such as Brook Bond tea company and Tata industries in steel and manufacturing, had introduced incentive payments for male sterilization since the mid-sixties as part of their fringe benefit plans. In 1966 some state governments started larger programs for promoting sterilization; they established camps where men could go for the operation and receive payment. These policies were also encouraged by the central government. In fact, the whole program and its local and central administrative support grew so much that it started to look like a compulsory policy. Local officials were rewarded according to the number of men sterilized. There is some evidence that insufficient checks were made on whether the men fulfilled all requirements to join the program and also whether they really understood what the operation meant, especially that it was permanent. The large monetary reward—in their eyes—could well have appeared irresistible for poor families and some actual compulsion is likely to have occurred. During fiscal year 1976–77 more than eight million sterilizations were performed, six million of them on males. This interference with personal privacy provoked strong reaction. Indira Gandhi's government was defeated in the 1977 election, the only time that her party has been defeated since the independence of the country. There were several reasons for this election result, but the sterilization program was credited as a major one. The next government abolished the program and since then elected governments have been wary of being accused of compulsion. Sterilization has decreased correspondingly: in 1983–84, four and a half million sterilizations were performed, but only six hundred thousand of them were on males. Despite the cultural norms against male sterilization, sterilization is still the most widely used method of contraception, including 30 percent of contraceptors (Government of India 1984).

The most extreme governmental action was undertaken in a totalitarian country, the People's Republic of China. In 1978 the government declared a definite policy on population stabilization and possibly reduction; to achieve this a norm of one child per family was established. China has a well-established welfare system: many necessities and amenities of life are allocated by the state, including housing, education, work assignments, food rations, and most components of income. Thus it is very easy to make life unpleasant for noncompliers. In addition, China had established a community-based system in which community units, such as villages and factories, make a contract with the state committing themselves to standards of production, ideology, and behavior in exchange for central support; this commitment is then enforced on members of the community by the political leaders. Compliance with family planning is included in the contract and the enforcement methods left to each unit (Kroll, Darrin, and Kane 1985, Tien 1980).

The allocation of children is thus bureaucratically controlled. Families who cooperate receive a one-child certificate, which entitles them to a number of privileges in the receipt of public goods. Party cadre and similarly responsible officials are expected to earn this certificate. The norm requires that there be special reasons for a second child, such as a defect in the first; in some villages a special certificate is needed for having a second child. Extreme methods of persuasion have been described for use on women who have violated the rules and become pregnant inappropriately, such as interminable group sessions with long harangues by cadre and other participants. These thought reform procedures are so overpowering that most women consent to abortion, even quite late in the term (Mosher 1983).

These techniques are easier to apply in the closed small communes in the countryside than in the more open cities although paradoxically the economic need for children is higher in the country. Throughout all this activity the government-sponsored planned parenthood association provides a network of support, information, appliances, and propagandists as well as possible supervision. This role goes beyond the limits that a voluntary social movement would assume.

The population program is not the only concern of the Chinese government, which also has an ambitious program of economic and social reform. Somewhat at cross-purpose with the population policy, the new direction includes increase in freedom of choice and economic self-determination in many ways and thus a general diminution of social control. The increase of the private sector gives discretionary income to families and makes them less dependent on public welfare policies; even home ownership, which is conducive to individual control of space and family size, is encouraged. The Chinese program has been quite successful in reducing the fertility rate, but it has not quite achieved its ultimate goal of one child per family, occasionally two and never more than that. In a situation the reverse of that in America, the gradual liberalization in China has slowed down the drive toward family planning. China must be the primary example of the transformation of the original libertarian aims of the family planning movement into new norms; it also exhibits, even under totalitarian condition, the limits that culture and perhaps human nature impose.

Comprehensive Understanding

The very demonstration of the movement's strength—international organization, the crisis atmosphere, and influence on governmental action—shows the complexity of the birth control issue. It has its foundations in biology, it includes conditions of the family and relations between the sexes, it must rely on the organization of medicine and public health, it is circumscribed by questions of morality and religion, and it becomes an important aspect of economic and political planning. Each new effort that deals with part of this complex may soon be stopped by opposition and by neglect of other important factors. This recurring history has led some scientists working in the field to propose integrative models that take into account a whole range of conditions. These theoretical efforts can become guidelines for comprehensive action and are therefore important for the movement at this stage of its development.

Even these comprehensive models are primarily concerned with just one of the two branches of concern: family planning and population control. Richard Easterlin's (1978) micro-economic model is an example of the family planning model. The worldwide introduction of family planning programs has generated a wealth of data on individual conditions and motives for having children and the resulting actions. The challenge here is to find a simple model that can incorporate different findings from a multitude of studies. Easterlin, an economist, designed his model by first distinguishing supply of children from demand for them. He defined supply of children by biological and cultural conditions in the society: if these conditions, such as diet, age at marriage, and sexual restraint, are set for a society, then supply is defined by the number of children reaching adulthood (conventionally taken as twenty years) that a couple would have in that society without trying to limit fertility. Demand, in Easterlin's terms, refers to the goals in family size that a family sets; it can be represented by the distribution of expenditure for children compared with other goods in a family's budget, given economic restraints. Demand therefore reflects general conditions as well as the value and cost of children, psychological as well as economic.

Supply and demand generally do not coincide: if supply exceeds demand—the situation with which the family planning movement is concerned—then the difference is made up by contraception; the outcome will be a point between supply of children and demand; its location will depend on the cost of contraception, which includes the financial cost, level of knowledge about birth control, availability, and social prohibitions. If the cost is high, fertility will equal the supply of children—children born in absence of contraception; if it is low, fertility will equal the demand—perfect family planning in a contracepting society.

Many social changes can be fit into this scheme, which explains how a certain mix of policies will produce contradictory results in fertility. The power of the model is shown in an extensive analysis of fertility in underdeveloped countries by the National Academy of Sciences, which studied varied aspects of fertility and family planning according to it (Bulatao and Lee 1983). Easterlin's model proposes that the original aim of the family planning movement can be seen as reduction of the cost of contraception. But some of the movement's other social aims, such as reduction of infant mortality, improvements in maternal health or better nutrition, would increase the supply of children, making contraception to reach a certain level of fertility more costly. The aim of many population control policies, especially noncoercive ones, was to reduce demand, but the psychological factors in the value of children involved in demand are more intricate. The complexities demonstrated by this model can explain many of the difficulties of family planning and can help to indicate advisable action based on an understanding of the whole social situation, preventing exclusive reliance on one kind of approach.

As the name *micro-economic* indicates, Easterlin's model derives from the actions of individuals and families. A population control model designed by Bernard Berelson (1978), on the other hand, tries to compare countries. Here the data are more limited: in contrast to the large number of individuals whose conditions and views of fertility one can obtain, here the units under discussion are whole countries, whose number is severely limited, even if one extends the discussion in time and uses past countries as well as present ones. In addition, the data needed for this analysis have not been universally collected.

Berelson, a social scientist, was president of the Population Council from 1966 to 1974; at this time many avenues in population control were opening up and he saw as his task to find rational means to channel the activities of the council most effectively. He distinguished four types of policy affecting fertility: family planning, development, formal community organizations, and direct governmental pressure. He applied the analysis of these policies to twenty-seven developing countries for which he had sufficient data: these countries were ranked according to the degree to which they had achieved a birth rate comparable to that of the industrialized countries: the "certain" ones who had almost done so, the "probable," which had clear tendencies in this direction, the "possible," which had shown some favorable conditions and the "unlikely," where all signs were unfavorable for achieving this goal.

This classification corresponds to the presence of the four types of policy. The "certain" have all four policies—family planning, development, community organization, and direct pressure—while the "unlikely" countries have none.

The important insights come from the transitional groups. The "probables" only lack family planning programs, while the "possibles" need also more specific measures in their development and community programs. This model shows that the family planning movement in the narrow sense is effective in the final stage of fertility decline, when all structural conditions are already met. If they are not present, than a family planning program with its clinics and case workers has little basis for its work.

Berelson shows where family planning can be most effective and where other policies, apparently removed from family planning, should have priority. The "probables" are the places where the international family planning movement would have its best successes; after all, the movement started in the Western countries when they were in the same conditions as the "probables" are now.

The activities of the family planning movement, its allies, and even its opponents become clearer when thus set in a framework by a scientist integrating all the different aspects of population theory. This junction of the pragmatic activities of the family planning activists and the theories of scientists indicates the present state of both fields. It can also give guideposts for the future of the family planning movement.

Chapter Ten

New Challenges

As the ideas of family planning and population control have become part of established wisdom, they also have become subject to new challenges. Now part of the accepted spectrum of social thought, family planning is discussed as part and parcel of any general position. But, in many ways, family planning is basically incompatible with conventional political divisions.

Limits of Population Control

By the Darwinian principle, the number of members of a species is the criterion of success of the species's adaptation to its environment. Applying this argument to the human species, population increase is a sign of success for humanity. Thus it would seem unreasonable to propose that humans, or any animal species, attempt to decrease population as a means of survival.

In 1962, however, at the height of the family planning movement, V. C. Wynne-Edwards, a biologist, made just this claim, demonstrating some mechanisms by which animal species do control their own fertility. He pointed to such phenomena as restriction of nesting sites and considered the displays of many species (such as the nightly swarming of birds and insects) to be rough censuses that show the participants' capacity for further expansion. Some of his theories have been influential in the work of population biology, which tries to integrate evolutionary biology, ethology, and demography; other of his theories, reflecting a social concern about population planning, may be exaggerated. Still other theories

147

indicate that not every individual member of a species tries to leave maximum offspring; one can look at colony-building insects—bees, ants—as specializing fertility in some members. The size of the colony is contained by the existence of nonprocreating members; this system creates a large but nonexpanding population (Dawkins 1976).

Probably the safest statement of our knowledge at the present time is that there may be some natural regulation of population size; it is true, for example, that we find little evidence of mass starvation of animals except under unusual catastrophic conditions (excessive droughts, very hard winters etc.). Regular starvation would be the case if lack of subsistence was the only limiting factor of population size. It is also possible that cultural development has led to a breakdown of some of these natural mechanisms in the human population, especially by removing human life from food production in the development of cities and technology. But, the same ingenuity that put humanity into this predicament should be able to rescue it as well.

This is the point at which a new approach to demography undercuts the support that demography has traditionally given to the family planning movement. This new direction is best represented by Julian Simon (1981), an economist. His argument is formulated and defended through intricate mathematical techniques but his central point is that the main economic resource is human ingenuity or brain power. For instance, the increase in energy production came through the discovery of the use of coal, steam power, oil, electricity, the internal combustion engine, and nuclear power, not through the additional discovery of previously accepted sources of energy. That is, the solution came through invention, not through exploitation of limited resources. Correspondingly, Simon argues, it is likely that a new energy crisis will be overcome through new ideas, not through exploitation of current energy sources. Increase in human ingenuity is in part a function of more people. Crudely speaking, the more brains, the more ideas possible. Further, ingenuity is frequently stimulated by hardships, such as population pressure, and thus the presence of real or imagined crises will lead to more thought about the problem and thus to new ways of benefiting humanity. In this way overpopulation will bring about its own solution over an extended period of time.

More formally, this argument may be distinguished from the conventional model of the effect of high fertility. This standard model assumes constant cultural and technological conditions and shows how increased population size will consume the products that the increased labor force can produce and, thus, that any population increase will negate any progress. Simon assumes that the technological conditions will depend in part on fertility and population increase itself. We cannot talk about the effects of fertility and economic well-being with the assumption that technology will stay constant, for rather than staying constant it is likely to improve with population pressure. In the cross-sectional picture that the traditional theory gives, fertility will hinder economic development. But over a longer time the lessons learned and the ingenuity exerted will lead to a better state of well-being. (Or, in technical language, the state of technology is an extrinsic variable in traditional population models and an intrinsic variable in Simon's model.)

Besides the econometric analysis general evidence gives plausibility to this theory. Much has been made of the abrupt rise of population since the industrial revolution; the total human population reached one billion a century and a half ago and increased to five billion by 1987. And there is certainly starvation and misery in many areas of the globe. Yet, it is likely that a smaller proportion of humanity lives in extreme poverty today; on the average, and for a greater proportion than before the rise of population, the standard of living has risen remarkably. What we call today the poverty line is a standard of living that would have been beyond the imagining for all except the most favored persons in the eighteenth century. Although it would be misleading to assert from these events that population increase leads to prosperity, they certainly make a case for the importance of human ingenuity. The conditions for improvement of inventiveness are an important consideration in economic development and this may include the challenge of population pressure.

Simon can also point to comparisons between different places. Certainly urban areas are among the wealthiest places in the world, and attract new residents for their better opportunities; also most intellectual and technological progress originates in densely settled places, suggesting population pressure as an incentive for creativity. These comparisons within countries may be misleading and confound cause and effect: perhaps the rewards of city life attract people with great potential. Nevertheless, similar comparisons can be made between political units. One of the most densely settled regions in the world, the Low Countries, has the highest standard of living; comparison on Hong Kong with the People's Republic of China and Singapore with Malaysia favors the densely settled, urban states. Certainly increase in population and high density by itself do not always lead to catastrophic results and a case can be made in their favor.

This new approach to political economy does not advocate unrestrained population increase; neither does it oppose family planning as such. Human ingenuity would also include putting the brakes on overpopulation when it becomes necessary. It only opposes emphasis on population control as a primary means of improving standards of living and asserts the importance of many other factors, which put population control into a larger framework; the optimum population size cannot be easily determined and one must trust future, wiser planners to reach a rational conclusion.

The Asian comparisons mentioned above show the importance of the economic system and the favorable climate of a market economy for economic development. The argument between advocates of the importance of economic system and overpopulation is reminiscent of the debate in Malthus's time: Senior asserted that industrial development under a free market would avoid the Malthusian dilemma; Marx and Engels attacked Malthus for giving excuses for the present system of distribution and claimed that socialism would open abundance to an ever increasing population.

This argument, especially as it was formulated by Simon, may be a portent of a future threat to the movement. It played an important role in the 1980s, because Simon was influential in the Reagan administration and was advisor to the U.S. delegation at the UN Mexico conference in 1984. One of the main issues at the meeting was the withholding of funds for activities that supported abortion. The possibility that this policy might endanger other family planning and population control activity would not seem important to a delegation that did not subscribe to the view that overpopulation is the primary threat (Brown 1984).

The absorption of the ideas of family planning into the norms of society came when the mainstream of demographers, sociologists, and economists became sensitive to dangers of overpopulation; family planning then became an integral part of national and international policy. If these social scientists start to abandon their antinatalist position, family planning will have to rely only upon individual motivations, as it did before the general fear of population explosion developed.

Population Control and Political Ideology

Opposition to the Malthusian argument persisted not only among the free market advocates, but among socialists as well. For them the dogma remained that the earth is sufficiently bountiful to support an extremely large population and that only an unjust social system leads to shortages and poverty. This view, however, turned out not to be completely prona-talist and opposed to the family planning movement. Several conditions contributed to this ambivalence. First of all, the pronounced separation from organized religion among Marxists erased any objection to specific contraceptive techniques. Thus, in principle, they supported freedom of choice in birth control as part of the general liberation of women and the working classes. Many early pioneers of the family planning movement were socialists of some sort, although the organized labor movement objected to incorporating support of birth control among its goals because it was seen as primarily a middle-class concern.

When Marxists assumed power in a number of countries following World War II they became subject to additional pressures, because of the needs of the state. On the one hand, the countries had need of a labor force, especially for rebuilding after a devastating war; there was even a need to make up population losses from the war. On the other hand, there were the familiar problems of overpopulation and the short-run effect of a large, economically dependent child population; furthermore, many socialist governments promoted radical changes in the organization of the family, especially emancipation of women from exclusive concern with home and children. The outcome of these conflicting pressures was an extreme fluctuation of policies, from strong encouragement of all man-ner of contraceptive measures, including the one-child policy in China, to social support for fertility and legal measures against contraception.

Just as the policies of Marxist led governments show a whole range of aims and means, a similar ambivalence is demonstrated in arguments initiated by left-wing groups in capitalist countries. Here the desire to provide government services for working-class women frequently clashes with suspicions of the aim of population control policies. This apparent inconsistency is another example of the difficulty of fitting family planning and population control into the conventional political spectrum.

Population Control and Less Developed Countries

In spite of the original affinity to radical, liberal, and socialist groups, the family planning movement has often been subject to attacks from part-ners in its erstwhile coalition. The most significant break has been over the relation of family planning to foreign aid programs, exactly the issue that population explosion activists wanted to tackle. Some dissident groups within the social science field attacked this connection, however, even any promotion of contraception with foreign aid, as vicious and as forcing developing countries to conform with the needs of the capitalist leaders of the industrialized countries. For instance, within the field of demography, a group called the Concerned Demographers published for a while a newsletter that cast doubts on the motives of the population control establishment. This attack was concentrated especially on the Population Council, partially because of its initial relation with the Rockefellers. The involvement of this family, the symbol of capitalist international enterprise, with international family planning was almost taken a prima facie evidence of ulterior designs. In addition, the support of large foundations, such as the Ford Foundation, added to the suspicion.

Stripped of the innuendos of conspiracy, the dissident economic argument is somewhat complicated. It has been presented succinctly by an anthropologist, Steven Polgar (1971). He points out that the countries that are now called "Third World" had been able to maintain a stable population until the coming of European colonialism. Polgar claims that the families did not have any motivation for an excessive number of children until the arrival of the colonialists who needed cheap labor for their large-scale enterprises. Thus the colonial rulers created conditions for high fertility. The claims by many population control activists that people in these countries want large families, is fallacious, Polgar argues; if we could restore integrity to the societies, then family planning would take care of itself. Efforts to impose contraception clash with present structural conditions of the societies, such as plantation and industrial labor, which the Western societies themselves instituted. Polgar was not opposed to family planning as such: he was for a time on the staff of the Planned Parenthood Federation. But he insisted that the real solution to overpopulation in certain countries rested in the change of underlying causes due to Western influence.

This point of view became quite popular, especially in the less developed countries themselves, and led the setback of the family planning movement at the UN Bucharest Conference in 1974. Here the final resolution gave developmental aid priority over instrumental support for family planning. The countries were allowed to claim economic aid first and then promote contraceptive policies, instead of having aid conditional on family planning as Hardin and Ehrlich proposed. This issue remains a sensitive one. Oxfam, an English private relief organization, provides family planning services as individual aid, but it condemns their use within a population control framework (Oxfam News 1987).

The conflicts in the two UN conferences, in 1974 and 1984, show the vulnerability of the family planning movement to attacks from the left and from the right. In Bucharest aid from the industrialized countries and planned development was put before family planning; in Mexico City opposition to abortion and trust in a free market hampered support for family planning. The results reflect the political climate of the two decades.

Minorities and Family Planning

The argument over whether family planning policies can assume the major responsibilities for population control or whether basic changes in the system are necessary rests on economic theories. But there is more sensitive question embedded in the debate: this is the question of *which* population is too large.

People are divided into ethnic, racial, religious, and other similar groups. Like separate species, they frequently want their group to be large, often for realistic concerns over power. Thus, attempting to restrict aid to poorer overpopulated countries can easily be seen as stating, "We are the right number, but we don't want any more of you." Open expression of this argument is usually avoided in international discussion, but it remains a mute presence, leading to caution on one side and resentment on the other. The family planning movement is limited by its presence and forced to act diplomatically on the international scene.

This discussion becomes more vehement within a society where minorities may feel threatened by contraceptive policies used as a weapon against them. Groups with few resources may feel that the power of numbers is the only way in which they can make their voice heard. Thus advocates of the poor, like Cesar Chavez, the leader of the United Farm Workers, encourage their followers to increase their number to obtain political power. As the poorer minorities are also the groups among which the family planning movement is active in field work and clinics, some conflict is likely to occur. Often family planning is seen by the poor as middle-class people trying to impose their values.

The difficulty in promoting family planning is exacerbated when this power difference is based on long-time racial conflict. The relation of Blacks to family planning is influenced by this tradition. The problem here is more serious because there is evidence of some illegitimate use of contraceptive techniques to keep down the Black population, especially in the use of sterilization and abortion. Several states have legalized involuntary sterilization under certain conditions; the manner in which safeguards are applied and the methods of persuasion used have shown some evidence of discrimination. The same suspicion, voiced especially by Black Muslims, rests on involuntary abortion, or abortion of which the woman is not aware at the time, such as during anaesthesia (Sarvis and Rodman 1973). Therefore, some Black leaders and organizations oppose the legality of abortions. Few, however support the right-to-life movement, because of disagreements on other political issues. Here we see again the incongruity of the family planning issue with conventional political divisions.

Sterilization and abortion are only the most extreme issues that concern Blacks; there is a general suspicion that population control means principally reduction of the Black population. For example, consider an exposition of the issue by Robert Murray (1977), a prominent Black scientist. He notes that twenty policies have been variously suggested for population control; he finds that practically all would be objectionable because they affect different socioeconomic groups in a different way: for instance, financial incentives are more effective for the poor. There remain only three policies on the list that are nondiscriminatory: (1) a general educational campaign for the general public on family limitation, (2) restructuring the family to make the small family rational, (3) compulsory education of children on problems of population excess. While these three are nondiscriminatory, Murray asserts, they would still run into opposition from some powerful Black groups: Black Catholics for religious reasons, and Black Muslims and Pan-Africanists for nationalistic reasons. In fact, studies have shown that Black race consciousness leads to rejection of all contraception, at least among males (Darity et al. 1971).

Family Planning and Feminism

If the principles of family planning and population control are carried to their ultimate logical conclusion, then they will inevitably conflict with many of the principles of other movements who generally support family planning aims. Of course, some compromises can be reached in actual practice. For example, while many social welfare policies essentially help increase of population—after all they are designed to better support human life—few people in the movement will seriously advocate such policies as abolishing free education or maternal benefits. This would be tactically unwise, splitting the movement from many liberals who had supported many of its aims. If the family planning movement is to enter politics with its own program, then it will have to face many concrete situations in which different values of this kind will have to be dealt with.

Probably the clearest conflict can be seen in family planning's relation to feminism. There has been traditionally a close connection between family planning and women's rights: birth control has been seen as the instrument of women's freedom to follow a life course of their own choice. But transition to new norms of population control may reverse the freedom of choice women have gained. Enforcement and even encouragement of low fertility standards would usurp again women's rights to their bodies. The Chinese one-child family policy with its concurrent semienforced abortion is a warning sign.

Conflicts over enforcement of family size goals loom mainly in the future, but the conflict over specific policies is closer at hand. Many policies advocated now by women's groups lie in the field of general social welfare, such as parental leave or employers' provision of day-care. These measures clearly try to enable women to pursue employment while having children. This obviously increases their freedom of choice but runs counter to a consistent population control policy. In the early 1970s, in her report to the Commission on Population and the American Future, the demographer Judith Blake called this situation the "feminist trap." By this she meant the effort of the women's movement to enable women to have a career while being subject to the same claim to motherhood that they experienced without the career. Thus the women's movement has been following a pronatalist policy just as much as its opponents who want to keep women at home, while a consistent population control policy would encourage choice between motherhood and career and reward the career choice.

Another divisive issue between the two movements, as we have seen, is the introduction of contraceptives, some of which feminists have viewed as exploitative experimentation on women. Feminists are skeptical about the emphasis on female contraceptives at all. Here different spokeswomen have used opposite positions: on the one side there is a claim to give control of contraception to women; other proponents feel that men escape responsibility and risks by emphasizing female contraceptives (Segal 1972). Especially the use of hormones for contraception—that is the birth control pill—has been attacked by feminists as exploitation by male physicians, researchers, and big business (Seaman and Seaman 1977). And the successful attack on IUDs in the United States was also seen as a women's rights issue.

These are the issues that the family planning movement will have to face in the future when its leaders and followers try to settle the importance of family planning and population control in their general social program. The movement has to deal with new competing and overlapping ideas and has to determine its place within a comprehensive sociopolitical framework.

Teenage Pregnancy

Not all the obstacles the movement encounters come in the form of competing ideologies. An outstanding problem for the organized movement is adolescent pregnancy. Contraception is a virtually universal practice in the United States, as in industrialized and Western nations as a whole. But certain pockets of failure remain; one of them is teenagers (National Research Council 1987). Adolescent pregnancy is particularly a problem because of the high expectations of the family planning movement. The early hope of the movement had been that free access to relevant information and devices would lead to optimally healthy sexual expression combined with prudent birth control. This has not occurred, however, among the youngest group: adolescent pregnancy and fertility, if not appreciably higher than in previous times, has not participated in the general decline. Contraceptives are used less by teenagers than by other age groups.

Thus the question of teenage pregnancy is currently an important social problem and one in which the family planning movement can be active. Here some of the old conflicts with which the movement has dealt are being replayed. As the persons under consideration are still minors, direct influence on motivation and even some partially coercive measures have ample precedent; this has traditionally included control of adolescent sex. But concern with this problem has coincided with a more permissive view of adolescent sexuality: yesterday's sexual delinquent is today's sexually active teenager. The idea is now sufficiently entrenched that any direct attack on adolescent sex will be strongly opposed, ridiculed, or declared impossibly impractical. The increase in adolescent sexual activity must be compensated by increased contraceptive use just to keep the pregnancy rate even.

For another contemporary value, however, adolescent pregnancy forms a direct threat. That is the high value placed on every person's, women as well as men, reaching as high an educational level as possible and having an occupational career. The threat of interruption of this life plan through pregnancy and childbearing makes adolescent fertility a prominent problem in contemporary society. The combination of sexual permissiveness and preparation for careers puts a great strain on teenagers, which adds to biological and social stresses of adolescence. This conflict in values makes normative influences difficult and leaves the solution to the traditional work of the family planning movement, namely the improvement of contraceptive use.

In the drive to reduce adolescent pregnancy the action of the planned parenthood organizations follow a familiar pattern: exposition of the deleterious effects of teenage pregnancy; work on public support for sex and contraceptive education, especially its adoption in the school curriculum; establishment of clinics and outreach in the critical communities. Even the debates of the old struggle remain: opponents claim that sex education in public schools offends general morality and also that it will increase sexual activity, thus being counterproductive. There is also some effort to restrict contraceptive services, especially abortion, for teenagers, or at least to make it dependent on parental notification and consent. The contest on these issues is fought through publicity and legislative and judicial action.

Here the family planning movement is staying in the familiar territory of introducing knowledge and behavior to a sector of the population to which these patterns are new; this sector has been left behind in the general social change that the movement has promoted. Thus family planners are back to the activity in which they have been so successful in the past: finding new ways to reach potential clients, fighting legal restrictions, and trying to overwhelm organized or traditional opposition. The "new" group is different from other new populations in that it is being introduced to sexual activity and associated developmental problems of adolescence. Thus family planning is being introduced to a group in a condition of emotional fragility and the effectiveness of a purely cognitive approach is questionable.

Instrumental Orientation

Work in this field is today mainly focused on the instrumental activity, the use of contraception and the knowledge of methods. Influence on sexual activity and even motivation for family planning is becoming less important. Social changes, which went beyond the power of the family planning movement, have modified the public attitude toward sexual behavior; in addition, this attitude has become part of the division between liberal and conservative ideology. Many of the tenets of conservative ideology run counter to the ideas of the family planning movement, and thus the movement is careful not to espouse parental control over adolescent sexual behavior or related restrictive sexual norms. This conflict is especially clear in the argument over abortion. The power of the right-to-life movement in conservative politics, particularly the influence it had on the Reagan administration, has militated against public support of abortion and, in consequence, of any organization that does provide abortion services. Strict interpretation of this policy has led to cutting off funds from national and international family planning services. It is understandable that other efforts connected with the conservative ideology will be viewed with suspicion by family planners.

It is possible, on the other hand, that a cyclic change may reduce sexual permissiveness and bring new motivational forces to bear on reduction of adolescent fertility; this change in social mores occurred in the transition from Regency England to Victorianism in the early nineteenth century and can be inferred in the change from the swinging 1960s to the conservative 80s. The family planning movement does not promote this social influence on motivation, perhaps because a dependence on large-scale social factors is repugnant to individually centered family planners. The other aspect of motivation, the emphasis on occupational careers, can be more easily combined with the instrumental approach, and has been tried with some success.

The main emphasis of the movement remains at present on contraceptive services, as shown in the budget of PPFA; even scientific meetings on family planning and related topics seem to define the topic as provision of services, their organization and their effect. This organization around contraception may restrict the fervor of movement advocacy and make family planning just another social service. This would mark another step in the gradual absorption of the family planning movement into the establishment, although it was the stated aim of many of the early advocates. Emphasis on contraception has, however, some inherent dangers; family planning risks being stalled if certain means become controversial. How the fight over abortion led to a countermovement with strong political impact, the right-to-life movement, is a good example of this.

Side effects of contraceptive devices can, however, lead to new situations that can be advantageous to the movement. A most recent example is the effect of the Acquired Immune Deficiency Syndrome (AIDS) epidemic. As the main emphasis on prevention of this disease is instrumental, the use of condoms, this birth control device has started to overcome taboos against its mention in mass media and advertising, just as the use of condoms in preventing venereal disease was permitted when sale of contraceptives was prohibited. The effects of this wide promotion of a contraceptive, even if not intended for birth control cannot be estimated at the present time. Another consequence of concern about AIDS is the growth of nonpermissive sexual norms, as expressed in appeals that restriction to one partner is the best means of prevention. Influence of these ideas may lead to motivational changes in contraception, for example among adolescents. On the other hand, the effects of AIDS on the family planning movement may be negative, because funds and efforts that have been devoted to family planning are being directed to the fight against AIDS. Similarly, unanticipated events may affect the future of population control and family planning, and thus make forecasts about the future of the movement difficult.

Conclusion

The family planning movement is an example of a movement whose principal aims have been accomplished. It was never the kind of movement that shakes a society by its roots, but it had an agenda that advocated new values, knowledge, and actions, previously unthinkable among most people. A socially innovative movement, it can serve as a convenient model to represent the workings of other, larger, social movements. It is also the model of a successful movement that must face the consequences of success.

To be sure, the goals of many activists in the movement included larger social and personal changes as the result of family planning. Many of these goals remain unfulfilled and hopes for their realization have kept the movement alive, at least its functioning organizations. Such aims as personal self-expression, improved personal relations between the sexes, joyous family life, and maintaining an optimum population level would need many additional social changes, if they are at all attainable outside utopian conditions or without heavy costs in other areas.

The history of the family planning movement has clearly demonstrated two important features of social movements: the interplay of individual and social factors and the different steps of development. In this movement the individual and social influences were distinct and even had separate aims: family planning and population control. Family planning arose to relieve individual distress, meet personal needs, and effect changes in behavior and outlook. Consequently, the persons who were active in this branch of the movement, especially at the beginning, had to engage themselves in visible and sometimes dangerous actions; the creation and fight for acceptance for birth control was the work of strong women and men. The history of the movement bears the imprint of their individual ideas and personalities. On the other hand, the gradual diffusion of the ideas of population control was the less spectacular work of scholars. This work was favored by a change in world conditions after World War II, when the principles of population control changed the entire social perspective and led to a climate in which family planning activity was not just tolerated, but actively welcomed. The work of the two branches met at the right time, which led to the success of the movement in an unexpectedly short period.

The first stage of the movement was a struggle against established rules of thought and action and emphasized the right to hold new views. When these views were incorporated into the mainstream of social thought, the movement had to assume a different function. One approach to cope with this situation has been to keep up the old work, especially in conditions where effective contraception is not practicable. This would include the defense of abortion and the continuing struggle against teenage pregnancy. Another approach has been to press for stronger links to established social platforms and make family and population planning a public responsibility. This makes family planning a political issue and thus vulnerable to political changes that are fundamentally unconnected with family planning issues. On the other hand, with these political links it could work toward achieving some of the wider aims that inspired the movement in its start. Finally, the movement can accept its success and not go beyond it. It can keep functioning as a recognized social agency and maintain its link with the medical profession.

We may expect the movement will resort to a combination of these possibilities. The nature of exact path to be taken will depend on the general social scene of the future; but, as in the past, it will be influenced by the nature of the people who reach positions of leadership in the movement and give it new ideas and strategies.

Chronology

1759	Francis Place born.
1766	Thomas Malthus born.
1789	French Revolution: impetus to radical and reform movements in Europe and North America.
1793	William Godwin's *Enquiry concerning Political Justice* published.
1798	Malthus publishes first edition of *Essay on Population,* introducing "Malthus's Law."
1803	Second edition of *Essay on Population* includes preventive checks.
1822	Place publishes *Illustrations and Proofs of the Principle of Population,* advocating contraception as preventive check.
1823	Place and Carlile publish "diabolical handbills."
1826	Nassau Senior attacks Malthus's population theory from a free market position in *Two Lectures on Population.*
1832	Knowlton's book *Fruits of Philosophy* published in U.S.
1834	Malthus dies.
1844	Marx and Engels attack the "myth of overpopulation" and Malthus's theory.
1854	Place dies.
1869	Emma Goldman born.
1872	Comstock Act passed, banning use of U.S. mail for distribution and information on contraception.

1877	Bradlaugh-Besant trial; revitalized Malthusian League founded.
1879	Margaret Sanger born.
1890	Marie Stopes born.
1900	Goldman returns to United States after training in contraception; combines anarchist and birth control activities.
1901	President William McKinley assassinated by anarchists; campaign against anarchists.
1910	Sanger's involvement in socialist and anarchist groups.
1912	Death of Nellie Sachs of attempted abortion (Sanger's "conversion experience").
1914–1916	Sanger's stay in Europe; influence of Havelock Ellis; expertise in birth control.
1915	National Birth Control League (later Voluntary Parenthood League) formed by Mary Ware Dennett; Dennett wins Supreme Court decision on distribution of sex education pamphlets without lascivious intent (break in Comstock Act).
1916	Sanger opens Brownsville clinic.
1917	United States enters World War I; anarchists concentrate on antiwar activities; Sanger breaks with anarchists.
1920	Women's Suffrage Amendment; Stopes's *Married Love* published in the United States.
1921	Sanger founds American Birth Control League; Stopes opens birth control clinic in London.
1923	Birth Control Clinical Research Bureau opens.
1927	World Population Conference.
1928	Warren Thompson proposes theory of demographic transition.
1929	Police raid on Margaret Sanger's clinic; extent of support becomes manifest.
1933	Franklin Delano Roosevelt elected president; New Deal period of government activism begins.

1935	PRERA in Puerto Rico starts government supported birth control clinics.
1936	*U.S. v. One Package* authorizes mail use for medically used contraceptives.
1939	Venereal Disease Control Act authorizes Public Health Service involvement in contraception for venereal disease control, especially in armed services.
1941	United States enters World War II.
1942	Planned Parenthood Federation of America unites different birth control organizations without Sanger and other pioneers.
1948	Rockefeller Foundation mission to Far East; first volume of Kinsey reports on human sex life published.
1952	Population Council founded; International Planned Parenthood Federation founded.
1957	Clarence Gamble founds Pathfinder Fund.
1958	Marie Stopes dies.
1959	Draper report on necessity of population planning in foreign aid; rejected by President Dwight Eisenhower.
1960	First birth control pill (Enovid) marketed.
1965	President Lyndon Johnson's Great Society starts new period of public activism: new offices supporting population control in Department of Health, Education, and Welfare, and Department of State; *Griswold v. Connecticut* enjoins states from prohibiting contraceptive services; UN Population Conference in Belgrade, first step to UN activities.
1966	Margaret Sanger dies.
1969	United Nations Fund for Population Activities inaugurated.
1970	Congress mandates family planning program ("Title X"). First candidates presented by Right-to-Life Party in New York.
1971	Congress exempts contraception from Comstock Act.
1970–1972	Commission on Population Growth and the American Future recommends policy of population control; endorsed by President Richard Nixon.

1973   *Roe v. Wade* legalizes abortion with some restrictions.

1974   UN Population Conference in Bucharest; emphasis on development.

1977   Supreme Court accepts Hyde Amendment right by Congress to limit financial support of abortion (*Maher v. Doe* and *Beal v. Roe*).

1980   Right-to-Life Party candidate for president obtains thirty-two thousand votes.

1984   UN Population Conference in Mexico City; conflict on U.S. stand against support for abortion and for free market development as population planning.

1985   United States withdraws support of IPPF (and UN agencies) because of possible use of funds for abortion.

Bibliography

This bibliography includes the references in the text. Some of the more important historical works were used for large sections, and no individual reference was made for each item used from this source. The references used in this way—the major sources for this research—are marked with an asterisk (*). References in the text indicate which sources were consulted for a series of events; no attempt was made to document every statement.

Alberoni, F. 1984. *Movement and Institution*. New York: Columbia University Press.

Ariès P. 1962. *Centuries of Childhood*. New York: Knopf.

Arney, W. P. 1982. *Power and Profession of Medicine*. Chicago: University of Chicago Press.

Back, K. W. 1987. "The Logic of Socially Innovative Movements." *Journal for the Theory of Social Behavior* 17:161–80.

———. 1988. Myth in the Lives of Leaders of Social Movements: The Case of the Family Planning Movement. Biography 11, no. 2 (1988):95–107.

Back, K. W., Hill, R., and Stycos, J. M. 1960. "Population Control in Puerto Rico: The Formal and Informal Framework." *Law and Contemporary Problems* 25:558–76. 1987.

Back, K. W., and Winsborough, H. H. 1968–69. "Population Policy: Opinions and Actions of Governments." *Public Opinion Quarterly* 32:634–45.

*Balfour, M.; Evers, R.; Notestein, F.; and Taeuber, I. P. 1950. *Public Health and Demography in the Far East*. New York: Rockefeller Foundation.

Banks, J. A. 1954. *Prosperity and Parenthood: A Study of Family Planning in Victorian England*. London: International Library of Sociology and Social Reconstruction.

Barnett, L. D. 1974. "Zero Population Growth, Inc.: A Second Study." *Biosocial Science* 6: 1–22.

———. 1982. *Population Policy and the U.S. Constitution*. Boston-The Hague: Kluver Nijhoff.

*Berelson, B. 1978. "Prospects and Programs for Fertility Reduction: What? Where?" *Population and Development Review* 4: 579–616.

Besant, A. 1877. *The Law of Population,* London: T. Fisher Unwin.

———. 1976. *Selections of Social and Political Pamphlets,* New York: Augustus McKoll.

Bhende, A. A., and Khanikar, T. 1982. *Principles of Population Studies.* 2d ed. Bombay: Himalaya Press.

Billings, E., and Westmore, A. 1980. *The Billings Method: Controlling Fertility without Drugs and Devices.* Melbourne, Australia: Annie O'Donovan.

Blake, J. 1961. *Family Structure in Jamaica: The Social Context of Reproduction.* New York: Free Press.

———. 1972. "Coercive Pronatalism and American Population Policy." In *Aspects of Population Policy,* edited by R. J. Parke, and C. Westoff. Washington, D.C.: U.S. Government Printing Office.

Blumer, H. 1946. "Collective Behavior." In *New Outline of Principles of Sociology,* edited by A. M. Lee. New York: Barnes & Noble.

Brown, G. F. 1984. "UN International Conference on Population, 1984." *Studies in Family Planning* 15: 296–301.

Bulatao R. 1979. *On the Nature of the Transition in the Value of Children.* Population Division Paper #60A. Honolulu: East-West Center.

Bulatao, R., and Fawcett, J. T. 1983. *Influence on Childbearing Intentions across the Fertility Career: Demography, Socio-Economic Factors and the Value of Children.* Population Division Paper #60F. Honolulu: East-West Center.

*Bulatao, R., and Lee, R. D., eds. 1983. *Determinants of Fertility in Developing Countries.* New York: Academic Press.

Bumpass, L. L. 1987. "The Risk of Unwanted Birth: The Changing Concept of Contraception and Sterilization in the U.S." *Population Studies* 41:347–64.

Caldwell, J., and Caldwell, P. 1986. *Limiting Population Growth and the Ford Foundation Contribution.* New York: Ford Foundation.

Carlile, R. 1826: *Every Woman's Book.* London: Carlile.

*Chandrasekar, S. 1981. *"A Dirty, Filthy, Book."* Berkeley: University of California Press.

Coale, A., and Watkins, S., eds. 1985. *The Decline of Population in Europe.* Princeton: Princeton University Press.

Commission on Population Growth and the American Future. 1972. *Population and the American Future.* Washington, D.C.: U.S. Government Printing Office.

Croll E.; Davin, D.; and Kane, P., eds. 1985. *China's One-Child Family Policy.* New York: St. Martin's Press.

Darity, W. A.; Turner, C. B.; and Thiebaux, H. J. 1971. "An Exploratory Study on Barriers to Family Planning: Race Consciousness and the Fear of

Black Genocide as a Basis." Paper presented at Ninth Annual Meeting, American Association of Planned Parenthood Physicians.

Darwin, C. 1969. *Autobiography*. New York: Norton. Originally published 1887.

———. 1967. *The Voyage of the Beagle*. New York: Museum of Natural History. Originally published 1839.

Davis, K., and Blake, J. 1956. "Social Structure and Fertility: An Analytical Framework." *Economic Development and Cultural Change* 4:211–35.

Dawkins, R. 1976. *The Selfish Gene*. New York: Oxford University Press.

Dennett, M. W. 1926. *Birth Control Laws: Shall We Keep Them, Change Them or Abolish Them?* New York: Frederick H. Hitchcock; Grafton Press.

Dinnage, R. 1986. *Amy Besant*. Harmondsworth, England: Penguin.

Douglas, E. T. 1979. *Margaret Sanger: Prophet for the Future*. New York: Holt, Rinehart & Winston.

Drinnon, R. 1961. *Rebel in Paradise*. Chicago: University of Chicago Press.

Drysdale, G. R. 1859 *Elements of Social Science: Physical, Sexual and Natural Religion*. London: Strand, Reprint ed. 1905.

*Easterlin, R. A. 1978. "The Economics and Sociology of Fertility: A Synthesis." In *Historical Studies of Changing Fertility*, edited by C. Tilly. Princeton: Princeton University Press.

Ehrlich, P. R. 1968. *The Population Bomb*. New York: Ballantine.

Ellis, H. 1939. *My Life*. Boston: Houghton Mifflin.

*Eversley, D. E. C. 1959. *Social Theories of Fertility and the Malthusian Debate*, Oxford: Clarendon Press.

Farley, J. W., and Leavitt, H. J. 1968. "Jamaica: Private Sector Distribution of Contraceptives," *Studies in Family Planning* 1, no. 33:11–12.

Fawcett, J. T. 1983. *Perceptions of the Value of Children: Satisfactions and Costs* in *Determinants of Fertility in Developing Countries*, edited by R. Bulatao and R. D. Lee. New York: Academic Press.

*Fawcett, J. T., and Chen, P. S. 1979. *Public Policy and Population Change in Singapore*. New York: Population Council.

Forrest, J. D. 1986. "The End of IUD Marketing in the U.S.: What Does it Mean to American Women?" *Family Planning Perspectives* 18:52.

Foucault, M. 1980. *A History of Sexuality*. Vol. 1, *Introduction*. New York: Random House.

Frank, L. 1984. *Dickens and the Romantic Self*. Lincoln: University of Nebraska Press.

Freedman, R., and Takeshita, J. Y. 1969. *Family Planning in Taiwan: An Experiment in Social Change*. Princeton: Princeton University Press.

*Fryer, P. 1965. *The Birth Controllers*. London: Secker & Warburg.

Gay, P. *Education of the Senses*. 1984. New York: Oxford University Press.

Glass, D. V. 1973. *Numbering the People*. Farnsborough, England: Saxon House.

Godwin, W. 1793. *Enquiry concerning Political Justice and Its Influence on Morals and Happiness.* Reprinted. 1946. Austin: University of Texas Press.

―――. 1820. *On Population: An Enquiry concerning the Power of Increase in the Numbers of Mankind, being an Answer to Mr. Malthus Essay on that Subject.* London: Longmans.

Goldman, E. 1931. *Living My Life.* New York: Knopf.

Government of India. 1984. *Family Welfare Planning in India, 1983–84.* New Delhi, India: Department of Health and Social Services.

Graunt, J. 1662. *Natural And Political Observations upon the Bills of Mortality.* London.

Grosskurth, P. 1951. *Havelock Ellis.* New York: Knopf.

*Gruening, E. 1973. *Many Battles: The Autobiography of Ernest Gruening.* New York: Norton.

*Hall, R. 1977. *Passionate Crusader: The Life of Marie Stopes.* New York: Harcourt, Brace, Jovanovic.

Handlin, O. 1951. *The Uprooted: The Epic Story of the Migration That Made the American People.* New York: Grosset & Dunlap.

Hardin, G. 1975. *Explaining the New Ethics for Survival: The Voyage of Spaceship Beagle.* Philadelphia: University of Pennsylvania Press.

―――. 1979 *Promethean Ethics.* Seattle: University of Washington Press.

Hardin G., and Bader, J. 1970. *Managing the Commons.* San Francisco: Freeman.

Harrison, J. F. C. 1969. *Robert Owen and the Owenites in Britain and America.* London: Routledge & Kegan Paul.

Hatt, P. 1952. *Backgrounds of Human Fertility in Puerto Rico.* Princeton: Princeton University Press.

Hermann, C. B.; Williamson, N. E.; McCann, M.; Janowitz, B.; Kennedy, R. F.; and Thapor, S. 1986. *Periodic Abstinence in Developing Countries.* Institute for Resource Development at Westinghouse.

Hill, R.; Stycos, J. M.; and Back, K. W. 1959. *The Family and Population Control.* Chapel Hill: University of North Carolina Press.

Himes, N. 1936. *Medical History of Contraception.* Baltimore: Johns Hopkins University Press.

International Planned Parenthood Federation. 1985. Annual Report.

―――. 1986–87. Annual Report.

Kelman, H. C. 1958. "Compliance, Conflict, and Internalization." *Journal of Conflict Resolution* 2:51–60.

*Kennedy, D. M. 1970. *Birth Control in America: The Career of Margaret Sanger.* New Haven: Yale University Press.

*Kevles, D. J. 1985. *In the Name of Eugenics: Genetics and the Uses of Human Heredity.* New York: Knopf.

Kinsey, A. C. 1948. *Sex Life of the Human Male.* New York: Saunders.

―――. 1954. *Sex Life of the Human Female.* New York: Saunders.

Lader, L. 1955. *The Margaret Sanger Story.* Reprint ed. 1977. Westport, Conn.: Greenwood Press.

Landy, D. 1960. *Childbearing Patterns in a Puerto Rico Lower Class Community.* Rio Piedras, P. R.: University of Puerto Rico Press.

Laslett, P. 1985. *The World We Have Lost.* 3d ed. New York: Scribners.

*Ledbetter, A. 1976. *A History of the Malthusian League.* Columbus: Ohio State University Press.

Lesthaege, R. J. 1977. *The Decline of Belgian Fertility, 1890–1970.* Princeton: Princeton University Press.

*Luker, K. 1984. *Abortion: The Politics of Motherhood.* Berkeley: University of California Press.

McCleary, G. F. 1953. *The Malthusian Population Theory.* London: Faber & Faber.

McKeown, J. 1976. *The Modern Rise of Population.* London: Arnold.

*McLaren, A. 1978. *Birth Control in Nineteenth Century England.* London: Croom Helm.

Malthus, R. T. 1798. *An Essay on the Principle of Population as it Affects the Future Improvement of Society.* Reprint ed. 1970. Harmondsworth, England: Penguin (the "first essay").

———. 1803. *An Essay on the Principles of Population* 2d ed. London: J. Johnson (the "second essay").

Marx, K. 1875. *Critique of the Gotha Program.* Reprint. 1953. In *Marx and Engels on Malthus.* by L. E. Meek, London: Lawrence Wishart.

Maude, A. 1924. *The Authorized Life of Marie Stopes.* London: Williams & Norgate.

Mauldin, W. P.; Choucri, N.; Notestein, F. W.; and Teitelbaum, M. 1974. "The World Population Conference and the Population Tribune," *Studies in Family Planning* 5, no. 12: 357–96.

Meek, L. E. 1953. *Marx and Engels on Malthus.* London: Lawrence & Wishart.

Millbank Memorial Fund. 1955. *Current Research on Human Fertility.* New York: Milbank.

Mosher, S. 1983. *Broken Earth: The Rural Chinese.* New York: Free Press.

*Murray, R. J., Jr. 1977. "The Ethical and Moral Values of Black Americans and Population Policies." In *Population Policy and Ethics: The American Experience,* edited by R. M. Veatch. New York: Irvington.

National Research Council. 1987. *Risking the Future: Adolescent Sexuality, Pregnancy and Childbearing.* Washington, D.C.: National Academy Press.

Nye, R. A. 1984. *Crime, Madness, and Politics in Modern France: The Medical Concept of National Decline.* Princeton: Princeton University Press.

Owen, R. D. 1830. *Moral Physiology: A Brief and Plain Treatise on the Population Question.* New York: Wright and Owen.

Oxfam News. 1987. Winter issue.

*Petersen, W. 1979. *Malthus.* Cambridge, Mass.: Harvard University Press.

170   *Family Planning and Population Control*

Place, F. 1822. *Illustrations and Proofs of the Principle of Population. Including an Examination of the Proposed Remedies of Mr. Malthus and a Reply to Mr. Godwin and Others.* Reprint ed. New York: Kelley, 1967.

————. 1972. *The Autobiography of Francis Place (1771–1854).* edited by Mary Thale. Cambridge: Cambridge University Press.

Polgar, S. 1971. *Culture and Population.* Cambridge, Mass.: Schenkman (Carolina Population Center, Monograph No. 9).

Pomeroy, W. B. 1982. *Dr. Kinsey and the Institute on Sex Research.* New Haven, Conn.: Yale University Press.

*****Population Council.** 1978. *A Chronicle of the First Twenty-Five Years. 1951–1976.* New York: Population Council.

Ramirez, F. J., and Stans, A. N. 1987. "The Ending of IUD Sales in the U.S.: What Are the International Implications?" *International Family Planning Perspectives* 13:71–79.

Raventhold, R. T. 1968. "The AID Population and Family Planning Program: Goals, Scope, and Progress." *Demography* 5:561–73.

*****Reed, J.** 1978. *From Private Vice to Public Virtue: The Birth Control Movement and American Society since 1830.* New York: Basic Books.

Rock, J. 1963. *The Time Has Come: A Catholic Doctor's Proposals to End the Battle over Birth Control.* New York: Knopf.

Rock, J., and Loth, D. 1949. *Voluntary Parenthood.* New York: Random House.

Rogers, E. 1973. *Communication Strategies for Family Planning.* New York: Free Press.

Ryder, N. B., and Westoff, C. I. 1971. *Reproduction in the U.S.* Princeton: Princeton University Press.

Salas, R., ed. 1985. *UNFPA: Twenty Years.* New York: UN Publisher.

Sanger, M. 1938. *An Autobiography.* New York: Norton.

Sarvis, B., and Rodman, H. 1973. *The Abortion Controversy.* New York, Columbia University Press.

Seaman, B., and Seaman, C. 1977. *Women And the Crisis in Sex Hormones.* New York: Rowson Associates.

Segal, S. J. 1972. "Contraceptive Research: A Male Chauvinist Plot?" *Family Planning Perspectives* 4 (3):21–25.

Senior, N. 1826. *Two Lectures on Population.* London: Saunders & Ollen. Reprint ed. New York: Kelley, 1966.

*****Simon, J.** 1981. *The Ultimate Resource.* Princeton: Princeton University Press.

Smelser, N. 1963. *Theory of Collective Behavior.* New York: Free Press.

*****Soloway, R. A.** 1982. *Birth Control and the Population Question in England. 1877–1930.* Chapel Hill: University of North Carolina Press.

Spengler, J. J. 1938. *France Faces Depopulation.* Durham, N.C.: Duke University Press.

*Spitzer, R. J. 1987. *The Right to Life Movement and Third Party Politics.* Westport, Conn: Greenwood Press.

Starr, P. 1982. *The Social Transformation of American Medicine.* New York: Basic Books.

Stopes, M. 1920. *Married Love.* New York: Critic and Guide. Originally published by A. C. Enfield, 1918.

————. 1923. *Early Days of Birth Control.* London: Putnam.

Stycos, J. M. 1955. *Family and Fertility in Puerto Rico: A Study of the Lower Income Group.* New York: Columbia University Press.

————. 1955. "Birth Control Clinics in Crowded Puerto Rico." In *Health, Culture and Community,* edited by B. Paul. New York: Russell Sage.

————. 1977. "Some Minority Opinions on Birth Control." In Veatch, R.M., editor. *Population Policies and Ethics: The American Experience.* New York: Irvington.

Stycos, J. M., and Back, K. W. 1965. *The Control of Human Fertility in Jamaica.* Ithaca, N. Y.: Cornell University Press.

Suitters, B. 1973. *Be Brave and Angry.* London: IPPF.

Thompson, W. 1929. "Population." *American Journal of Sociology* 34:959–75.

Tien, H. Y., ed. 1980. *Population Theory in China.* White Plains, N. Y.: Sharpe.

Tugwell, R. 1946. *The Stricken Land: The Story of Puerto Rico.* Reprint ed. Westport, Conn.: Greenwood Press, 1968.

United Nations Fund for Population Activities (UNFPA). 1985. *Population Perspectives: Statements by World Leaders.* New York: United Nations.

Wallas, G. 1918. *The Life of Francis Place, 1771–1857.* London: Allen & Unwin.

Whelpton, P. K., and Kiser, C. V., eds. 1946–58. *Social Psychological Factors Affection Fertility* Vols. 1–5. New York: Milbank Memorial Fund.

Williams D., and Williams, C. 1978. *Every Child a Wanted Child: Clarence J. Gamble, His Work in the Birth Control Movement.* Cambridge, Mass.: Francis A. Courtney Library of Medicine.

Wood, C., and Suitters, B. 1970. *The Fight for Acceptance.* Aylesbury, England: MTP.

Wynne-Edwards, V. C. 1962. *Animal Behavior in Relation to Social Behavior.* Edinburgh: Olivier & Boyd.

Zatuchni, G. I.; Goldsmith, A.; and Sciarra, J. I. 1985. *Intra-Uterine Contraception: Advances and Future Prospects.* Philadelphia: Harper & Row.

Index